WILLIAM SHAKESPEARE

THE MERCHANT OF VENICE

CLASSICS

Published 2024

FiNGERPRINT! CLASSICS
Prakash Books

Fingerprint Publishing
@FingerprintP
@fingerprintpublishingbooks
www.fingerprintpublishing.com

ISBN: 978 93 8993 102 0

William Shakespeare began his career as an actor, writer, and part owner of a playing company called the Lord Chamberlain's Men, later known as King's Men, in London. Often regarded as the 'Bard of Avon' he is one of the world's pre-eminent dramatists. Born and brought up in Stratford-upon-Avon, he married Anne Hathaway at the age of eighteen and they had three children—Susanna, and twins Hamnet and Judith. Though few records survive of his private life, he appeared to have retired to Stratford around 1613 where he died three years later.

His works still in existence, including some collaborations, consist of thirty-eight plays, one hundred and fifty-four sonnets, two long narrative poems, and several other verses. His plays are performed much more than any other playwright's and have been translated in almost all major languages. Most of his known works have been produced between 1589 and 1613. His early plays were mainly comedies and histories which remain regarded as some of the best works produced in these genres.

Shakespeare's plays are difficult to date. His early classical and Italianate comedies contain tight double plots and precise comic sequences giving way to the romantic atmosphere of his most acclaimed comedies in the mid-1590s. *A Midsummer Night's Dream*—a witty mixture of romance, fairy magic, and comic low life scenes—is one of his most delightful creations shortly before he turned to *Romeo and Juliet*. *Romeo and Juliet* is his most famous romantic tragedy of sexually charged adolescence, love, and death. It marks a departure from his earlier works and from others of the English Renaissance.

His plays demonstrate the expansiveness of his imagination and the extent of his learning. Shakespeare's sequence of great comedies continues with *Merchant of Venice*, *Much Ado About Nothing*, *As You Like It*, and *Twelfth Night*. Exploring the themes of bigotry, prejudice, justice, and humanity, *Merchant of Venice* is considered an anti-Semitic work. The play continues to remain one of his great comedies.

Shakespeare introduced prose comedy in the histories of the late 1590s—*Henry IV, Part I* and *Part II*, and *Henry V*—after the lyrical *Richard II*. *Julius Caesar* introduced a new kind of drama. Based on true events from Roman history, it is one of Shakespeare's most loved political tragedies.

Shakespeare wrote the so-called 'problem plays' in the early 17th century. *Measure for Measure, Troilus and Cressida*, and *All's Well that Ends Well* being a few of them. Until about 1608, he mainly wrote tragedies including *Hamlet, Othello, King Lear*, and *Macbeth*.

Antony and Cleopatra and *Coriolanus*—his last major tragedies, contain some of his finest poetry. Shakespeare wrote tragicomedies, also known as romances, in his last phase. These include *Cymbeline, The Winter's Tale*, and *The Tempest*, as well as the collaboration *Pericles, Prince of Tyre*.

A true genius, Shakespeare's popular characters and plots are studied, performed, reinterpreted, and discussed till today. William Shakespeare, known as the English national poet, is considered the greatest dramatist of all time.

CHARACTERS OF THE PLAY

THE DUKE OF VENICE
THE PRINCE OF MOROCCO ⎱
THE PRINCE OF ARRAGON ⎰ suitors to Portia
ANTONIO, a merchant of Venice
BASSANIO, his friend
SALANIO ⎱
SALARINO ⎬ friends to Antonio and Bassanio
GRATIANO ⎰
LORENZO, in love with Jessica
SHYLOCK, a rich Jew
TUBAL, a Jew, his friend
LAUNCELOT GOBBO, a clown, servant to
Shylock
OLD GOBBO, father to Launcelot
LEONARDO, servant to Bassanio
BALTHASAR ⎱ servants to Portia
STEPHANO ⎰

PORTIA, a rich heiress
NERISSA, her waiting-maid
JESSICA, daughter to Shylock
Magnificoes of Venice, Officers of the Court of Justice,
Gaoler, Servants to Portia, and other Attendants.

SCENE:
PARTLY AT VENICE, AND PARTLY AT BELMONT, THE SEAT OF PORTIA, ON THE CONTINENT

Act I

SCENE I. VENICE. A STREET

Enter ANTONIO, SALARINO, and SALANIO

ANTONIO

    In sooth, I know not why I am so sad;
    It wearies me; you say it wearies you;
    But how I caught it, found it, or came by it,
    What stuff 'tis made of, whereof it is born,
    I am to learn;
    And such a want-wit sadness makes of me
    That I have much ado to know myself.

SALARINO

    Your mind is tossing on the ocean;
    There where your argosies, with portly sail—
    Like signiors and rich burghers on the flood,
    Or as it were the pageants of the sea—
    Do overpeer the petty traffickers,

That curtsy to them, do them reverence,
As they fly by them with their woven wings.

SALANIO

Believe me, sir, had I such venture forth,
The better part of my affections would
Be with my hopes abroad. I should be still
Plucking the grass to know where sits the wind,
Peering in maps for ports, and piers, and roads;
And every object that might make me fear
Misfortune to my ventures, out of doubt
Would make me sad.

SALARINO

My wind, cooling my broth
Would blow me to an ague, when I thought
What harm a wind too great might do at sea.
I should not see the sandy hour-glass run
But I should think of shallows and of flats,
And see my wealthy Andrew dock'd in sand,
Vailing her high top lower than her ribs
To kiss her burial. Should I go to church
And see the holy edifice of stone,
And not bethink me straight of dangerous
    rocks,
Which, touching but my gentle vessel's side,
Would scatter all her spices on the stream,
Enrobe the roaring waters with my silks,
And, in a word, but even now worth this,

And now worth nothing? Shall I have the
    thought
To think on this, and shall I lack the thought
That such a thing bechanc'd would make me
    sad?
But tell not me; I know Antonio
Is sad to think upon his merchandise.

ANTONIO

Believe me, no; I thank my fortune for it,
My ventures are not in one bottom trusted,
Nor to one place; nor is my whole estate
Upon the fortune of this present year;
Therefore my merchandise makes me not sad.

SALARINO

Why, then you are in love.

ANTONIO

Fie, fie!

SALARINO

Not in love neither? Then let us say you are sad
Because you are not merry; and 'twere as easy
For you to laugh and leap and say you are merry,
Because you are not sad. Now, by two-headed
    Janus,
Nature hath fram'd strange fellows in her time:
Some that will evermore peep through their eyes,
And laugh like parrots at a bag-piper;
And other of such vinegar aspect

That they'll not show their teeth in way of smile
Though Nestor swear the jest be laughable.

Enter BASSANIO, LORENZO,
and GRATIANO

SALANIO

Here comes Bassanio, your most noble kinsman,
Gratiano, and Lorenzo. Fare ye well;
We leave you now with better company.

SALARINO

I would have stay'd till I had made you merry,
If worthier friends had not prevented me.

ANTONIO

Your worth is very dear in my regard.
I take it your own business calls on you,
And you embrace th' occasion to depart.

SALARINO

Good morrow, my good lords.

BASSANIO

Good signiors both, when shall we laugh? Say
when.
You grow exceeding strange; must it be so?

SALARINO

We'll make our leisures to attend on yours.

Exeunt SALARINO and
SALANIO

LORENZO

My Lord Bassanio, since you have found
Antonio,
We two will leave you; but at dinner-time,
I pray you, have in mind where we must meet.

BASSANIO

I will not fail you.

GRATIANO

You look not well, Signior Antonio;
You have too much respect upon the world;
They lose it that do buy it with much care.
Believe me, you are marvellously chang'd.

ANTONIO

I hold the world but as the world, Gratiano;
A stage, where every man must play a part,
And mine a sad one.

GRATIANO

Let me play the fool;
With mirth and laughter let old wrinkles come;
And let my liver rather heat with wine
Than my heart cool with mortifying groans.
Why should a man whose blood is warm within
Sit like his grandsire cut in alabaster,
Sleep when he wakes, and creep into the jaundice
By being peevish? I tell thee what, Antonio—
I love thee, and 'tis my love that speaks—

There are a sort of men whose visages
Do cream and mantle like a standing pond,
And do a wilful stillness entertain,
With purpose to be dress'd in an opinion
Of wisdom, gravity, profound conceit;
As who should say 'I am Sir Oracle,
And when I ope my lips let no dog bark.'
O my Antonio, I do know of these
That therefore only are reputed wise
For saying nothing; when, I am very sure,
If they should speak, would almost damn
    those ears
Which, hearing them, would call their brothers
    fools.
I'll tell thee more of this another time.
But fish not with this melancholy bait,
For this fool gudgeon, this opinion.
Come, good Lorenzo. Fare ye well awhile;
I'll end my exhortation after dinner.

LORENZO

Well, we will leave you then till dinner-time.
I must be one of these same dumb wise men,
For Gratiano never lets me speak.

GRATIANO

Well, keep me company but two years moe,
Thou shalt not know the sound of thine own
    tongue.

ANTONIO

Fare you well; I'll grow a talker for this gear.

GRATIANO

Thanks, i' faith, for silence is only commendable
In a neat's tongue dried, and a maid not vendible.

Exeunt GRATIANO and
LORENZO

ANTONIO

Is that anything now?

BASSANIO

Gratiano speaks an infinite deal of nothing,
more than any man in all Venice. His reasons
are as two grains of wheat hid in, two bushels
of chaff: you shall seek all day ere you find
them, and when you have them they are not
worth the search.

ANTONIO

Well; tell me now what lady is the same
To whom you swore a secret pilgrimage,
That you to-day promis'd to tell me of?

BASSANIO

'Tis not unknown to you, Antonio,
How much I have disabled mine estate
By something showing a more swelling port
Than my faint means would grant continuance;
Nor do I now make moan to be abridg'd
From such a noble rate; but my chief care

17

Is to come fairly off from the great debts
Wherein my time, something too prodigal,
Hath left me gag'd. To you, Antonio,
I owe the most, in money and in love;
And from your love I have a warranty
To unburden all my plots and purposes
How to get clear of all the debts I owe.

ANTONIO

I pray you, good Bassanio, let me know it;
And if it stand, as you yourself still do,
Within the eye of honour, be assur'd
My purse, my person, my extremest means,
Lie all unlock'd to your occasions.

BASSANIO

In my school-days, when I had lost one shaft,
I shot his fellow of the self-same flight
The self-same way, with more advised watch,
To find the other forth; and by adventuring both
I oft found both. I urge this childhood proof,
Because what follows is pure innocence.
I owe you much; and, like a wilful youth,
That which I owe is lost; but if you please
To shoot another arrow that self way
Which you did shoot the first, I do not doubt,
As I will watch the aim, or to find both,
Or bring your latter hazard back again
And thankfully rest debtor for the first.

ANTONIO

You know me well, and herein spend but time
To wind about my love with circumstance;
And out of doubt you do me now more wrong
In making question of my uttermost
Than if you had made waste of all I have.
Then do but say to me what I should do
That in your knowledge may by me be done,
And I am prest unto it; therefore, speak.

BASSANIO

In Belmont is a lady richly left,
And she is fair and, fairer than that word,
Of wondrous virtues. Sometimes from her eyes
I did receive fair speechless messages:
Her name is Portia—nothing undervalu'd
To Cato's daughter, Brutus' Portia:
Nor is the wide world ignorant of her worth,
For the four winds blow in from every coast
Renowned suitors, and her sunny locks
Hang on her temples like a golden fleece;
Which makes her seat of Belmont Colchos'
    strond,
And many Jasons come in quest of her.
O my Antonio! had I but the means
To hold a rival place with one of them,
I have a mind presages me such thrift
That I should questionless be fortunate.

ANTONIO

Thou know'st that all my fortunes are at sea;
Neither have I money nor commodity
To raise a present sum; therefore go forth,
Try what my credit can in Venice do;
That shall be rack'd, even to the uttermost,
To furnish thee to Belmont to fair Portia.
Go presently inquire, and so will I,
Where money is; and I no question make
To have it of my trust or for my sake.

Exeunt

SCENE II. BELMONT. A ROOM IN PORTIA'S HOUSE

Enter PORTIA and NERISSA

PORTIA

By my troth, Nerissa, my little body is aweary
of this great world.

NERISSA

You would be, sweet madam, if your miseries
were in the same abundance as your good
fortunes are; and yet, for aught I see, they are as
sick that surfeit with too much as they that starve
with nothing. It is no mean happiness, therefore,
to be seated in the mean: superfluity come sooner
by white hairs, but competency lives longer.

PORTIA

Good sentences, and well pronounced.

NERISSA

They would be better, if well followed.

PORTIA

If to do were as easy as to know what were good to do, chapels had been churches, and poor men's cottages princes' palaces. It is a good divine that follows his own instructions; I can easier teach twenty what were good to be done than to be one of the twenty to follow mine own teaching. The brain may devise laws for the blood, but a hot temper leaps o'er a cold decree; such a hare is madness the youth, to skip o'er the meshes of good counsel the cripple. But this reasoning is not in the fashion to choose me a husband. O me, the word 'choose'! I may neither choose who I would nor refuse who I dislike; so is the will of a living daughter curb'd by the will of a dead father. Is it not hard, Nerissa, that I cannot choose one, nor refuse none?

NERISSA

Your father was ever virtuous, and holy men at their death have good inspirations; therefore the lott'ry that he hath devised in these three chests, of gold, silver, and lead, whereof who chooses his meaning chooses you, will no doubt never be chosen by any rightly but one who you shall rightly love. But what warmth is there in your affection towards any of these princely suitors that are already come?

PORTIA

I pray thee over-name them; and as thou namest them, I will describe them; and according to my description, level at my affection.

NERISSA

First, there is the Neapolitan prince.

PORTIA

Ay, that's a colt indeed, for he doth nothing but talk of his horse; and he makes it a great appropriation to his own good parts that he can shoe him himself; I am much afeard my lady his mother play'd false with a smith.

NERISSA

Then is there the County Palatine.

PORTIA

He doth nothing but frown, as who should say 'An you will not have me, choose.' He hears merry tales and smiles not: I fear he will prove the weeping philosopher when he grows old, being so full of unmannerly sadness in his youth. I had rather be married to a death's-head with a bone in his mouth than to either of these. God defend me from these two!

NERISSA

How say you by the French lord, Monsieur Le Bon?

PORTIA

God made him, and therefore let him pass for a man. In truth, I know it is a sin to be a mocker, but he! why, he hath a horse better than the Neapolitan's, a better bad habit of frowning than the Count Palatine; he is every man in no man. If a throstle sing he falls straight a-capering; he will fence with his own shadow; if I should marry him, I should marry twenty husbands. If he would despise me, I would forgive him; for if he love me to madness, I shall never requite him.

NERISSA

What say you, then, to Falconbridge, the young baron of England?

PORTIA

You know I say nothing to him, for he understands not me, nor I him: he hath neither Latin, French, nor Italian, and you will come into the court and swear that I have a poor pennyworth in the English. He is a proper man's picture; but alas, who can converse with a dumb-show? How oddly he is suited! I think he bought his doublet in Italy, his round hose in France, his bonnet in Germany, and his behaviour everywhere.

NERISSA

What think you of the Scottish lord, his neighbour?

PORTIA

That he hath a neighbourly charity in him, for he borrowed a box of the ear of the Englishman, and swore he would pay him again when he was able; I think the Frenchman became his surety, and sealed under for another.

NERISSA

How like you the young German, the Duke of Saxony's nephew?

PORTIA

Very vilely in the morning when he is sober, and most vilely in the afternoon when he is drunk: when he is best, he is a little worse than a man, and when he is worst, he is little better than a beast. An the worst fall that ever fell, I hope I shall make shift to go without him.

NERISSA

If he should offer to choose, and choose the right casket, you should refuse to perform your father's will, if you should refuse to accept him.

PORTIA

Therefore, for fear of the worst, I pray thee set a deep glass of Rhenish wine on the contrary casket; for if the devil be within and that temptation without, I know he will choose it. I will do anything, Nerissa, ere I will be married to a sponge.

NERISSA

You need not fear, lady, the having any of these lords; they have acquainted me with their determinations, which is indeed to return to their home, and to trouble you with no more suit, unless you may be won by some other sort than your father's imposition, depending on the caskets.

PORTIA

If I live to be as old as Sibylla, I will die as chaste as Diana, unless I be obtained by the manner of my father's will. I am glad this parcel of wooers are so reasonable; for there is not one among them but I dote on his very absence, and I pray God grant them a fair departure.

NERISSA

Do you not remember, lady, in your father's time, a Venetian, a scholar and a soldier, that came hither in company of the Marquis of Montferrat?

PORTIA

Yes, yes, it was Bassanio; as I think, so was he called.

NERISSA

True, madam; he, of all the men that ever my foolish eyes looked upon, was the best deserving a fair lady.

PORTIA

I remember him well, and I remember him worthy of thy praise.

Enter a SERVANT

How now! what news?

SERVANT

The four strangers seek for you, madam, to take their leave; and there is a forerunner come from a fifth, the Prince of Morocco, who brings word the Prince his master will be here to-night.

PORTIA

If I could bid the fifth welcome with so good heart as I can bid the other four farewell, I should be glad of his approach; if he have the condition of a saint and the complexion of a devil, I had rather he should shrive me than wive me. Come, Nerissa. Sirrah, go before. Whiles we shut the gate upon one wooer, another knocks at the door.

Exeunt

SCENE III. VENICE. A PUBLIC PLACE

Enter BASSANIO and SHYLOCK

SHYLOCK

Three thousand ducats; well?

BASSANIO

Ay, sir, for three months.

SHYLOCK

For three months; well?

BASSANIO

For the which, as I told you, Antonio shall be bound.

SHYLOCK

Antonio shall become bound; well?

BASSANIO

May you stead me? Will you pleasure me? Shall I know your answer?

SHYLOCK

Three thousand ducats, for three months, and Antonio bound.

BASSANIO

Your answer to that.

SHYLOCK

Antonio is a good man.

BASSANIO

Have you heard any imputation to the contrary?

SHYLOCK

Ho, no, no, no, no: my meaning in saying he is a good man is to have you understand me that he is sufficient; yet his means are in supposition: he hath an argosy bound to Tripolis, another to the Indies; I understand, moreover, upon the Rialto, he hath a third at Mexico, a fourth for England, and other ventures he hath, squandered abroad. But ships are but boards, sailors but men; there be land-rats and water-rats, land-thieves and water-thieves—I mean pirates; and then there is the peril of waters, winds, and rocks. The man is, notwithstanding, sufficient. Three thousand ducats— I think I may take his bond.

BASSANIO

Be assured you may.

SHYLOCK

I will be assured I may; and, that I may be assured, I will bethink me. May I speak with Antonio?

BASSANIO

If it please you to dine with us.

SHYLOCK

Yes, to smell pork; to eat of the habitation which your prophet, the Nazarite, conjured the devil into. I will buy with you, sell with you,

talk with you, walk with you, and so following;
but I will not eat with you, drink with you, nor
pray with you. What news on the Rialto? Who
is he comes here?

Enter ANTONIO

BASSANIO

This is Signior Antonio.

SHYLOCK

[*Aside*] How like a fawning publican he looks!
I hate him for he is a Christian;
But more for that in low simplicity
He lends out money gratis, and brings down
The rate of usance here with us in Venice.
If I can catch him once upon the hip,
I will feed fat the ancient grudge I bear him.
He hates our sacred nation; and he rails,
Even there where merchants most do
	congregate,
On me, my bargains, and my well-won thrift,
Which he calls interest. Cursed be my tribe
If I forgive him!

BASSANIO

Shylock, do you hear?

SHYLOCK

I am debating of my present store,
And, by the near guess of my memory,
I cannot instantly raise up the gross

Of full three thousand ducats. What of that?
Tubal, a wealthy Hebrew of my tribe,
Will furnish me. But soft! how many months
Do you desire? [*To ANTONIO*] Rest you fair,
    good signior;
Your worship was the last man in our mouths.

ANTONIO

Shylock, albeit I neither lend nor borrow
By taking nor by giving of excess,
Yet, to supply the ripe wants of my friend,
I'll break a custom. [*To BASSANIO*] Is he yet
    possess'd
How much ye would?

SHYLOCK

Ay, ay, three thousand ducats.

ANTONIO

And for three months.

SHYLOCK

I had forgot; three months; you told me so.
Well then, your bond; and, let me see. But hear
    you,
Methought you said you neither lend nor borrow
Upon advantage.

ANTONIO

I do never use it.

SHYLOCK

When Jacob graz'd his uncle Laban's sheep—

This Jacob from our holy Abram was,
As his wise mother wrought in his behalf,
The third possessor; ay, he was the third—

ANTONIO

And what of him? Did he take interest?

SHYLOCK

No, not take interest; not, as you would say,
Directly interest; mark what Jacob did.
When Laban and himself were compromis'd
That all the eanlings which were streak'd and
    pied
Should fall as Jacob's hire, the ewes, being rank,
In end of autumn turned to the rams;
And when the work of generation was
Between these woolly breeders in the act,
The skilful shepherd pill'd me certain wands,
And, in the doing of the deed of kind,
He stuck them up before the fulsome ewes,
Who, then conceiving, did in eaning time
Fall parti-colour'd lambs, and those were
    Jacob's.
This was a way to thrive, and he was blest;
And thrift is blessing, if men steal it not.

ANTONIO

This was a venture, sir, that Jacob serv'd for;
A thing not in his power to bring to pass,
But sway'd and fashion'd by the hand of heaven.

Was this inserted to make interest good?

Or is your gold and silver ewes and rams?

SHYLOCK

I cannot tell; I make it breed as fast.

But note me, signior.

ANTONIO

Mark you this, Bassanio,

The devil can cite Scripture for his purpose.

An evil soul producing holy witness

Is like a villain with a smiling cheek,

A goodly apple rotten at the heart.

O, what a goodly outside falsehood hath!

SHYLOCK

Three thousand ducats; 'tis a good round sum.

Three months from twelve; then let me see the
rate.

ANTONIO

Well, Shylock, shall we be beholding to you?

SHYLOCK

Signior Antonio, many a time and oft

In the Rialto you have rated me

About my moneys and my usances;

Still have I borne it with a patient shrug,

For suff'rance is the badge of all our tribe;

You call me misbeliever, cut-throat dog,

And spit upon my Jewish gaberdine,

And all for use of that which is mine own.

Well then, it now appears you need my help;
Go to, then; you come to me, and you say
'Shylock, we would have moneys.' You say so:
You that did void your rheum upon my beard,
And foot me as you spurn a stranger cur
Over your threshold; moneys is your suit.
What should I say to you? Should I not say
'Hath a dog money? Is it possible
A cur can lend three thousand ducats?' Or
Shall I bend low and, in a bondman's key,
With bated breath and whisp'ring humbleness,
Say this:—
'Fair sir, you spit on me on Wednesday last;
You spurn'd me such a day; another time
You call'd me dog; and for these courtesies
I'll lend you thus much moneys?'

ANTONIO

I am as like to call thee so again,
To spit on thee again, to spurn thee too.
If thou wilt lend this money, lend it not
As to thy friends—for when did friendship take
A breed for barren metal of his friend?—
But lend it rather to thine enemy,
Who if he break thou mayst with better face
Exact the penalty.

SHYLOCK

Why, look you, how you storm!

33

I would be friends with you, and have your love,
Forget the shames that you have stain'd me with,
Supply your present wants, and take no doit
Of usance for my moneys, and you'll not hear
     me:
This is kind I offer.

BASSANIO

This were kindness.

SHYLOCK

This kindness will I show.
Go with me to a notary, seal me there
Your single bond; and, in a merry sport,
If you repay me not on such a day,
In such a place, such sum or sums as are
Express'd in the condition, let the forfeit
Be nominated for an equal pound
Of your fair flesh, to be cut off and taken
In what part of your body pleaseth me.

ANTONIO

Content, in faith; I'll seal to such a bond,
And say there is much kindness in the Jew.

BASSANIO

You shall not seal to such a bond for me;
I'll rather dwell in my necessity.

ANTONIO

Why, fear not, man; I will not forfeit it;
Within these two months, that's a month before

This bond expires, I do expect return
Of thrice three times the value of this bond.

SHYLOCK

O father Abram, what these Christians are,
Whose own hard dealings teaches them suspect
The thoughts of others. Pray you, tell me this;
If he should break his day, what should I gain
By the exaction of the forfeiture?
A pound of man's flesh, taken from a man,
Is not so estimable, profitable neither,
As flesh of muttons, beefs, or goats. I say,
To buy his favour, I extend this friendship;
If he will take it, so; if not, adieu;
And, for my love, I pray you wrong me not.

ANTONIO

Yes, Shylock, I will seal unto this bond.

SHYLOCK

Then meet me forthwith at the notary's;
Give him direction for this merry bond,
And I will go and purse the ducats straight,
See to my house, left in the fearful guard
Of an unthrifty knave, and presently
I'll be with you.

ANTONIO

Hie thee, gentle Jew.

Exit SHYLOCK

This Hebrew will turn Christian: he grows kind.

BASSANIO

I like not fair terms and a villain's mind.

ANTONIO

Come on; in this there can be no dismay;
My ships come home a month before the day.

Exeunt

Act II

SCENE I. BELMONT. A ROOM IN PORTIA'S HOUSE

Flourish of cornets. Enter the PRINCE OF MOROCCO, and his Followers; PORTIA, NERISSA, and Others of her train

PRINCE OF MOROCCO

Mislike me not for my complexion,
The shadow'd livery of the burnish'd sun,
To whom I am a neighbour, and near bred.
Bring me the fairest creature northward born,
Where Phoebus' fire scarce thaws the icicles,
And let us make incision for your love
To prove whose blood is reddest, his or mine.
I tell thee, lady, this aspect of mine
Hath fear'd the valiant; by my love, I swear
The best-regarded virgins of our clime

Have lov'd it too. I would not change this hue,
  Except to steal your thoughts, my gentle queen.

PORTIA

  In terms of choice I am not solely led
  By nice direction of a maiden's eyes;
  Besides, the lottery of my destiny
  Bars me the right of voluntary choosing;
  But, if my father had not scanted me
  And hedg'd me by his wit, to yield myself
  His wife who wins me by that means I told you,
  Yourself, renowned Prince, then stood as fair
  As any comer I have look'd on yet
  For my affection.

PRINCE OF MOROCCO

  Even for that I thank you:
  Therefore, I pray you, lead me to the caskets
  To try my fortune. By this scimitar,
  That slew the Sophy and a Persian prince,
  That won three fields of Sultan Solyman,
  I would o'erstare the sternest eyes that look,
  Outbrave the heart most daring on the earth,
  Pluck the young sucking cubs from the she-bear,
  Yea, mock the lion when he roars for prey,
  To win thee, lady. But, alas the while!
  If Hercules and Lichas play at dice
  Which is the better man, the greater throw
  May turn by fortune from the weaker hand.

So is Alcides beaten by his page;
And so may I, blind Fortune leading me,
Miss that which one unworthier may attain,
And die with grieving.

PORTIA

You must take your chance,
And either not attempt to choose at all,
Or swear before you choose, if you choose
wrong,
Never to speak to lady afterward
In way of marriage; therefore be advis'd.

PRINCE OF MOROCCO

Nor will not; come, bring me unto my chance.

PORTIA

First, forward to the temple: after dinner
Your hazard shall be made.

PRINCE OF MOROCCO

Good fortune then!
To make me blest or cursed'st among men!

Cornets, and Exeunt

SCENE II. VENICE. A STREET

Enter LAUNCELOT GOBBO
LAUNCELOT

Certainly my conscience will serve me to run from this Jew my master. The fiend is at mine elbow and tempts me, saying to me 'Gobbo, Launcelot Gobbo, good Launcelot' or 'good Gobbo' or 'good Launcelot Gobbo, use your legs, take the start, run away.' My conscience says 'No; take heed, honest Launcelot, take heed, honest Gobbo' or, as aforesaid, 'honest Launcelot Gobbo, do not run; scorn running with thy heels.' Well, the most courageous fiend bids me pack. 'Via!' says the fiend; 'away!' says the fiend. 'For the heavens, rouse up a brave mind,' says the fiend 'and run.' Well, my conscience, hanging about the neck of my heart, says very wisely to me 'My honest friend Launcelot, being an honest man's son'—or rather 'an honest woman's son'; for indeed my father did something smack, something grow to, he had a kind of taste—well, my conscience says 'Launcelot, budge not.' 'Budge,' says the fiend. 'Budge not,' says my conscience. 'Conscience,' say I, 'you counsel well.' 'Fiend,' say I, 'you counsel well.' To be

ruled by my conscience, I should stay with the
Jew my master, who—God bless the mark!—
is a kind of devil; and, to run away from the
Jew, I should be ruled by the fiend, who—
saving your reverence!—is the devil himself.
Certainly the Jew is the very devil incarnation;
and, in my conscience, my conscience is but a
kind of hard conscience, to offer to counsel me
to stay with the Jew. The fiend gives the more
friendly counsel: I will run, fiend; my heels are
at your commandment; I will run.

Enter OLD GOBBO, with a basket

OLD GOBBO

Master young man, you, I pray you; which is
the way to Master Jew's?

LAUNCELOT

[*Aside*] O heavens! This is my true-begotten
father, who, being more than sand-blind,
high-gravel blind, knows me not: I will try
confusions with him.

OLD GOBBO

Master young gentleman, I pray you, which is
the way to Master Jew's?

LAUNCELOT

Turn up on your right hand at the next turning,
but, at the next turning of all, on your left;
marry, at the very next turning, turn of no

41

hand, but turn down indirectly to the Jew's
house.

OLD GOBBO

Be God's sonties, 'twill be a hard way to hit.
Can you tell me whether one Launcelot, that
dwells with him, dwell with him or no?

LAUNCELOT

Talk you of young Master Launcelot? [*Aside*]
Mark me now; now will I raise the waters. Talk
you of young Master Launcelot?

OLD GOBBO

No master, sir, but a poor man's son; his father,
though I say't, is an honest exceeding poor
man, and, God be thanked, well to live.

LAUNCELOT

Well, let his father be what a will, we talk of
young Master Launcelot.

OLD GOBBO

Your worship's friend, and Launcelot, sir.

LAUNCELOT

But I pray you, ergo, old man, ergo, I beseech
you, talk you of young Master Launcelot?

OLD GOBBO

Of Launcelot, an't please your mastership.

LAUNCELOT

Ergo, Master Launcelot. Talk not of Master
Launcelot, father; for the young gentleman,

according to Fates and Destinies and such odd
sayings, the Sisters Three and such branches of
learning, is indeed deceased; or, as you would
say in plain terms, gone to heaven.

OLD GOBBO

Marry, God forbid! The boy was the very staff
of my age, my very prop.

LAUNCELOT

Do I look like a cudgel or a hovelpost, a staff
or a prop? Do you know me, father?

OLD GOBBO

Alack the day! I know you not, young
gentleman; but I pray you tell me, is my boy—
God rest his soul!—alive or dead?

LAUNCELOT

Do you not know me, father?

OLD GOBBO

Alack, sir, I am sand-blind; I know you not.

LAUNCELOT

Nay, indeed, if you had your eyes, you might
fail of the knowing me: it is a wise father that
knows his own child. Well, old man, I will tell
you news of your son. Give me your blessing;
truth will come to light; murder cannot be hid
long; a man's son may, but in the end truth
will out.

OLD GOBBO

Pray you, sir, stand up; I am sure you are not Launcelot, my boy.

LAUNCELOT

Pray you, let's have no more fooling about it, but give me your blessing; I am Launcelot, your boy that was, your son that is, your child that shall be.

OLD GOBBO

I cannot think you are my son.

LAUNCELOT

I know not what I shall think of that; but I am Launcelot, the Jew's man, and I am sure Margery your wife is my mother.

OLD GOBBO

Her name is Margery, indeed. I'll be sworn, if thou be Launcelot, thou art mine own flesh and blood. Lord worshipped might he be, what a beard hast thou got! Thou hast got more hair on thy chin than Dobbin my thill-horse has on his tail.

LAUNCELOT

It should seem, then, that Dobbin's tail grows backward; I am sure he had more hair on his tail than I have on my face when I last saw him.

OLD GOBBO

Lord! how art thou changed! How dost thou

and thy master agree? I have brought him a
present. How 'gree you now?

LAUNCELOT

Well, well; but, for mine own part, as I have set
up my rest to run away, so I will not rest till I have
run some ground. My master's a very Jew. Give
him a present! Give him a halter. I am famished
in his service; you may tell every finger I have
with my ribs. Father, I am glad you are come; give
me your present to one Master Bassanio, who
indeed gives rare new liveries. If I serve not him,
I will run as far as God has any ground. O rare
fortune! Here comes the man: to him, father; for
I am a Jew, if I serve the Jew any longer.

Enter BASSANIO, with LEONARDO,
with other Followers

BASSANIO

You may do so; but let it be so hasted that
supper be ready at the farthest by five of the
clock. See these letters delivered, put the
liveries to making, and desire Gratiano to
come anon to my lodging.

Exit a SERVANT

LAUNCELOT

To him, father.

OLD GOBBO

God bless your worship!

BASSANIO

Gramercy; wouldst thou aught with me?

OLD GOBBO

Here's my son, sir, a poor boy—

LAUNCELOT

Not a poor boy, sir, but the rich Jew's man, that would, sir, as my father shall specify—

OLD GOBBO

He hath a great infection, sir, as one would say, to serve—

LAUNCELOT

Indeed the short and the long is, I serve the Jew, and have a desire, as my father shall specify—

OLD GOBBO

His master and he, saving your worship's reverence, are scarce cater-cousins—

LAUNCELOT

To be brief, the very truth is that the Jew, having done me wrong, doth cause me, as my father, being I hope an old man, shall frutify unto you—

OLD GOBBO

I have here a dish of doves that I would bestow upon your worship; and my suit is—

LAUNCELOT

In very brief, the suit is impertinent to myself, as your worship shall know by this honest old

man; and, though I say it, though old man, yet
poor man, my father.

BASSANIO

One speak for both. What would you?

LAUNCELOT

Serve you, sir.

OLD GOBBO

That is the very defect of the matter, sir.

BASSANIO

I know thee well; thou hast obtain'd thy suit.
Shylock thy master spoke with me this day,
And hath preferr'd thee, if it be preferment
To leave a rich Jew's service to become
The follower of so poor a gentleman.

LAUNCELOT

The old proverb is very well parted between
my master Shylock and you, sir: you have the
grace of God, sir, and he hath enough.

BASSANIO

Thou speak'st it well. Go, father, with thy son.
Take leave of thy old master, and inquire
My lodging out. [*To a SERVANT*] Give him
    a livery
More guarded than his fellows'; see it done.

LAUNCELOT

Father, in. I cannot get a service, no! I have
ne'er a tongue in my head! [*Looking on his palm*]

Well; if any man in Italy have a fairer table
which doth offer to swear upon a book, I
shall have good fortune. Go to; here's a simple
line of life: here's a small trifle of wives; alas,
fifteen wives is nothing; a'leven widows and
nine maids is a simple coming-in for one man.
And then to scape drowning thrice, and to be
in peril of my life with the edge of a feather-
bed; here are simple scapes. Well, if Fortune
be a woman, she's a good wench for this gear.
Father, come; I'll take my leave of the Jew in
the twinkling of an eye.

Exeunt LAUNCELOT and
OLD GOBBO

BASSANIO

I pray thee, good Leonardo, think on this:
These things being bought and orderly bestow'd,
Return in haste, for I do feast to-night
My best esteem'd acquaintance; hie thee, go.

LEONARDO

My best endeavours shall be done herein.

Enter GRATIANO

GRATIANO

Where's your master?

LEONARDO

Yonder, sir, he walks.

Exit

GRATIANO

Signior Bassanio!

BASSANIO

Gratiano!

GRATIANO

I have suit to you.

BASSANIO

You have obtain'd it.

GRATIANO

You must not deny me: I must go with you to
Belmont.

BASSANIO

Why, then you must. But hear thee, Gratiano;
Thou art too wild, too rude, and bold of voice;
Parts that become thee happily enough,
And in such eyes as ours appear not faults;
But where thou art not known, why there they
show
Something too liberal. Pray thee, take pain
To allay with some cold drops of modesty
Thy skipping spirit, lest through thy wild
behaviour
I be misconstrued in the place I go to,
And lose my hopes.

GRATIANO

Signior Bassanio, hear me:
If I do not put on a sober habit,

Talk with respect, and swear but now and then,
Wear prayer-books in my pocket, look demurely,
Nay more, while grace is saying, hood mine eyes
Thus with my hat, and sigh, and say 'amen';
Use all the observance of civility,
Like one well studied in a sad ostent
To please his grandam, never trust me more.

BASSANIO

Well, we shall see your bearing.

GRATIANO

Nay, but I bar to-night; you shall not gauge me
By what we do to-night.

BASSANIO

No, that were pity;
I would entreat you rather to put on
Your boldest suit of mirth, for we have friends
That purpose merriment. But fare you well;
I have some business.

GRATIANO

And I must to Lorenzo and the rest;
But we will visit you at supper-time.

Exeunt

SCENE III. VENICE. A ROOM IN SHYLOCK'S HOUSE

Enter JESSICA and LAUNCELOT

JESSICA

I am sorry thou wilt leave my father so:
Our house is hell, and thou, a merry devil,
Didst rob it of some taste of tediousness.
But fare thee well; there is a ducat for thee;
And, Launcelot, soon at supper shalt thou see
Lorenzo, who is thy new master's guest:
Give him this letter; do it secretly.
And so farewell. I would not have my father
See me in talk with thee.

LAUNCELOT

Adieu! tears exhibit my tongue. Most beautiful
pagan, most sweet Jew! If a Christian do
not play the knave and get thee, I am much
deceived. But, adieu! these foolish drops do
something drown my manly spirit; adieu!

JESSICA

Farewell, good Launcelot.

Exit LAUNCELOT

Alack, what heinous sin is it in me
To be asham'd to be my father's child!
But though I am a daughter to his blood,
I am not to his manners. O Lorenzo!

If thou keep promise, I shall end this strife,
Become a Christian and thy loving wife.

Exit

SCENE IV. VENICE. A STREET

Enter GRATIANO, LORENZO, SALARINO, and SALANIO

LORENZO

Nay, we will slink away in supper-time,
Disguise us at my lodging, and return
All in an hour.

GRATIANO

We have not made good preparation.

SALARINO

We have not spoke us yet of torch-bearers.

SALANIO

'Tis vile, unless it may be quaintly order'd,
And better in my mind not undertook.

LORENZO

'Tis now but four o'clock; we have two hours
To furnish us.

Enter LAUNCELOT, with a letter

Friend Launcelot, what's the news?

LAUNCELOT

An it shall please you to break up this, it shall
seem to signify.

LORENZO

    I know the hand; in faith, 'tis a fair hand,

    And whiter than the paper it writ on

    Is the fair hand that writ.

GRATIANO

    Love news, in faith.

LAUNCELOT

    By your leave, sir.

LORENZO

    Whither goest thou?

LAUNCELOT

    Marry, sir, to bid my old master, the Jew, to sup

    to-night with my new master, the Christian.

LORENZO

    Hold, here, take this. Tell gentle Jessica

    I will not fail her; speak it privately.

    Go, gentlemen,

Exit LAUNCELOT

    Will you prepare you for this masque to-night?

    I am provided of a torch-bearer.

SALARINO

    Ay, marry, I'll be gone about it straight.

SALANIO

    And so will I.

LORENZO

    Meet me and Gratiano

    At Gratiano's lodging some hour hence.

SALARINO

'Tis good we do so.

Exeunt SALARINO and
SALANIO

GRATIANO

Was not that letter from fair Jessica?

LORENZO

I must needs tell thee all. She hath directed
How I shall take her from her father's house;
What gold and jewels she is furnish'd with;
What page's suit she hath in readiness.
If e'er the Jew her father come to heaven,
It will be for his gentle daughter's sake;
And never dare misfortune cross her foot,
Unless she do it under this excuse,
That she is issue to a faithless Jew.
Come, go with me, peruse this as thou goest;
Fair Jessica shall be my torch-bearer.

Exeunt

SCENE V. VENICE.
BEFORE SHYLOCK'S HOUSE

Enter SHYLOCK and LAUNCELOT

SHYLOCK

Well, thou shalt see; thy eyes shall be thy judge,
The difference of old Shylock and Bassanio:—
What, Jessica!—Thou shalt not gormandize,
As thou hast done with me—What, Jessica!—
And sleep and snore, and rend apparel out—
Why, Jessica, I say!

LAUNCELOT

Why, Jessica!

SHYLOCK

Who bids thee call? I do not bid thee call.

LAUNCELOT

Your worship was wont to tell me I could do
nothing without bidding.

Enter JESSICA

JESSICA

Call you? What is your will?

SHYLOCK

I am bid forth to supper, Jessica:
There are my keys. But wherefore should I go?
I am not bid for love; they flatter me;
But yet I'll go in hate, to feed upon
The prodigal Christian. Jessica, my girl,

Look to my house. I am right loath to go;
There is some ill a-brewing towards my rest,
For I did dream of money-bags to-night.

LAUNCELOT

I beseech you, sir, go: my young master doth
expect your reproach.

SHYLOCK

So do I his.

LAUNCELOT

And they have conspired together; I will not
say you shall see a masque, but if you do,
then it was not for nothing that my nose fell
a-bleeding on Black Monday last at six o'clock
i' the morning, falling out that year on Ash
Wednesday was four year in the afternoon.

SHYLOCK

What! are there masques? Hear you me, Jessica:
Lock up my doors, and when you hear the drum,
And the vile squealing of the wry-neck'd fife,
Clamber not you up to the casements then,
Nor thrust your head into the public street
To gaze on Christian fools with varnish'd faces;
But stop my house's ears—I mean my casements;
Let not the sound of shallow fopp'ry enter
My sober house. By Jacob's staff, I swear
I have no mind of feasting forth to-night;

But I will go. Go you before me, sirrah;
Say I will come.

LAUNCELOT

I will go before, sir. Mistress, look out at
window for all this;

There will come a Christian by
Will be worth a Jewess' eye.

Exit LAUNCELOT

SHYLOCK

What says that fool of Hagar's offspring, ha?

JESSICA

His words were 'Farewell, mistress'; nothing
else.

SHYLOCK

The patch is kind enough, but a huge feeder;
Snail-slow in profit, and he sleeps by day
More than the wild-cat; drones hive not with me,
Therefore I part with him; and part with him
To one that I would have him help to waste
His borrow'd purse. Well, Jessica, go in;
Perhaps I will return immediately:
Do I bid you, shut doors after you:
'Fast bind, fast find,'
A proverb never stale in thrifty mind.

Exit

JESSICA

Farewell; and if my fortune be not crost,
I have a father, you a daughter, lost.

Exit

SCENE VI. VENICE.
BEFORE SHYLOCK'S HOUSE

Enter GRATIANO and SALARINO, masqued

GRATIANO

This is the pent-house under which Lorenzo
Desir'd us to make stand.

SALARINO

His hour is almost past.

GRATIANO

And it is marvel he out-dwells his hour,
For lovers ever run before the clock.

SALARINO

O! ten times faster Venus' pigeons fly
To seal love's bonds new made than they are wont
To keep obliged faith unforfeited!

GRATIANO

That ever holds: who riseth from a feast
With that keen appetite that he sits down?
Where is the horse that doth untread again
His tedious measures with the unbated fire
That he did pace them first? All things that are

Are with more spirit chased than enjoy'd.
How like a younker or a prodigal
The scarfed bark puts from her native bay,
Hugg'd and embraced by the strumpet wind!
How like the prodigal doth she return,
With over-weather'd ribs and ragged sails,
Lean, rent, and beggar'd by the strumpet wind!

SALARINO

Here comes Lorenzo; more of this hereafter.

Enter LORENZO

LORENZO

Sweet friends, your patience for my long abode;
Not I, but my affairs, have made you wait:
When you shall please to play the thieves for
    wives,
I'll watch as long for you then. Approach;
Here dwells my father Jew. Ho! who's within?

Enter JESSICA, above, in boy's clothes

JESSICA

Who are you? Tell me, for more certainty,
Albeit I'll swear that I do know your tongue.

LORENZO

Lorenzo, and thy love.

JESSICA

Lorenzo, certain; and my love indeed,
For who love I so much? And now who knows
But you, Lorenzo, whether I am yours?

LORENZO

Heaven and thy thoughts are witness that
thou art.

JESSICA

Here, catch this casket; it is worth the pains.
I am glad 'tis night, you do not look on me,
For I am much asham'd of my exchange;
But love is blind, and lovers cannot see
The pretty follies that themselves commit,
For, if they could, Cupid himself would blush
To see me thus transformed to a boy.

LORENZO

Descend, for you must be my torch-bearer.

JESSICA

What! must I hold a candle to my shames?
They in themselves, good sooth, are too too
light.
Why, 'tis an office of discovery, love,
And I should be obscur'd.

LORENZO

So are you, sweet,
Even in the lovely garnish of a boy.
But come at once;
For the close night doth play the runaway,
And we are stay'd for at Bassanio's feast.

JESSICA

I will make fast the doors, and gild myself

With some moe ducats, and be with you straight.

Exit above

GRATIANO

Now, by my hood, a Gentile, and no Jew.

LORENZO

Beshrew me, but I love her heartily;

For she is wise, if I can judge of her,

And fair she is, if that mine eyes be true,

And true she is, as she hath prov'd herself;

And therefore, like herself, wise, fair, and true,

Shall she be placed in my constant soul.

Enter JESSICA

What, art thou come? On, gentlemen, away!

Our masquing mates by this time for us stay.

Exit with JESSICA and
SALARINO

Enter ANTONIO

ANTONIO

Who's there?

GRATIANO

Signior Antonio!

ANTONIO

Fie, fie, Gratiano! where are all the rest?

'Tis nine o'clock; our friends all stay for you.

No masque to-night: the wind is come about;

Bassanio presently will go aboard:

I have sent twenty out to seek for you.

GRATIANO

    I am glad on't: I desire no more delight

    Than to be under sail and gone to-night.

Exeunt

SCENE VII. BELMONT.
A ROOM IN PORTIA'S HOUSE

Flourish of cornets. Enter PORTIA, with the PRINCE
OF MOROCCO, and their trains

PORTIA

    Go draw aside the curtains and discover

    The several caskets to this noble prince.

    Now make your choice.

PRINCE OF MOROCCO

    The first, of gold, who this inscription bears:

    'Who chooseth me shall gain what many men
        desire.'

    The second, silver, which this promise carries:

    'Who chooseth me shall get as much as he deserves.'

    This third, dull lead, with warning all as blunt:

    'Who chooseth me must give and hazard all he
        hath.'

    How shall I know if I do choose the right?

PORTIA

    The one of them contains my picture, prince;

    If you choose that, then I am yours withal.

PRINCE OF MOROCCO

Some god direct my judgment! Let me see;
I will survey the inscriptions back again.
What says this leaden casket?
'Who chooseth me must give and hazard all he
hath.'
Must give: for what? For lead? Hazard for lead!
This casket threatens; men that hazard all
Do it in hope of fair advantages:
A golden mind stoops not to shows of dross;
I'll then nor give nor hazard aught for lead.
What says the silver with her virgin hue?
'Who chooseth me shall get as much as he
deserves.'
As much as he deserves! Pause there, Morocco,
And weigh thy value with an even hand.
If thou be'st rated by thy estimation,
Thou dost deserve enough, and yet enough
May not extend so far as to the lady;
And yet to be afeard of my deserving
Were but a weak disabling of myself.
As much as I deserve? Why, that's the lady!
I do in birth deserve her, and in fortunes,
In graces, and in qualities of breeding;
But more than these, in love I do deserve.
What if I stray'd no farther, but chose here?
Let's see once more this saying grav'd in gold:

'Who chooseth me shall gain what many men
    desire.'
Why, that's the lady: all the world desires her;
From the four corners of the earth they come,
To kiss this shrine, this mortal-breathing saint:
The Hyrcanian deserts and the vasty wilds
Of wide Arabia are as throughfares now
For princes to come view fair Portia:
The watery kingdom, whose ambitious head
Spits in the face of heaven, is no bar
To stop the foreign spirits, but they come
As o'er a brook to see fair Portia.
One of these three contains her heavenly
    picture.
Is't like that lead contains her? 'Twere damnation
To think so base a thought; it were too gross
To rib her cerecloth in the obscure grave.
Or shall I think in silver she's immur'd,
Being ten times undervalu'd to tried gold?
O sinful thought! Never so rich a gem
Was set in worse than gold. They have in
    England
A coin that bears the figure of an angel
Stamped in gold; but that's insculp'd upon;
But here an angel in a golden bed
Lies all within. Deliver me the key;
Here do I choose, and thrive I as I may!

PORTIA

There, take it, prince, and if my form lie there,
Then I am yours.
[*He unlocks the golden casket.*]

PRINCE OF MOROCCO

O hell! what have we here?
A carrion Death, within whose empty eye
There is a written scroll! I'll read the writing.
    'All that glisters is not gold,
    Often have you heard that told;
    Many a man his life hath sold
    But my outside to behold:
    Gilded tombs do worms infold.
    Had you been as wise as bold,
    Young in limbs, in judgment old,
    Your answer had not been inscroll'd:
    Fare you well, your suit is cold.'
Cold indeed; and labour lost:
Then, farewell, heat, and welcome, frost!
Portia, adieu! I have too griev'd a heart
To take a tedious leave; thus losers part.

            Exit with his train.
            Flourish of cornets

PORTIA

A gentle riddance. Draw the curtains: go.
Let all of his complexion choose me so.

            Exeunt

SCENE VIII. VENICE. A STREET

Enter SALARINO and SALANIO

SALARINO

    Why, man, I saw Bassanio under sail;

    With him is Gratiano gone along;

    And in their ship I am sure Lorenzo is not.

SALANIO

    The villain Jew with outcries rais'd the Duke,

    Who went with him to search Bassanio's ship.

SALARINO

    He came too late, the ship was under sail;

    But there the Duke was given to understand

    That in a gondola were seen together

    Lorenzo and his amorous Jessica.

    Besides, Antonio certified the Duke

    They were not with Bassanio in his ship.

SALANIO

    I never heard a passion so confus'd,

    So strange, outrageous, and so variable,

    As the dog Jew did utter in the streets.

    'My daughter! O my ducats! O my daughter!

    Fled with a Christian! O my Christian ducats!

    Justice! the law! my ducats and my daughter!

    A sealed bag, two sealed bags of ducats,

    Of double ducats, stol'n from me by my

        daughter!

And jewels! two stones, two rich and precious
    stones,
Stol'n by my daughter! Justice! find the girl!
She hath the stones upon her and the ducats.'

SALARINO

Why, all the boys in Venice follow him,
Crying, his stones, his daughter, and his ducats.

SALANIO

Let good Antonio look he keep his day,
Or he shall pay for this.

SALARINO

Marry, well remember'd.
I reason'd with a Frenchman yesterday,
Who told me—in the narrow seas that part
The French and English—there miscarried
A vessel of our country richly fraught.
I thought upon Antonio when he told me,
And wish'd in silence that it were not his.

SALANIO

You were best to tell Antonio what you hear;
Yet do not suddenly, for it may grieve him.

SALARINO

A kinder gentleman treads not the earth.
I saw Bassanio and Antonio part:
Bassanio told him he would make some speed
Of his return. He answer'd 'Do not so;
Slubber not business for my sake, Bassanio,

But stay the very riping of the time;
And for the Jew's bond which he hath of me,
Let it not enter in your mind of love:
Be merry, and employ your chiefest thoughts
To courtship, and such fair ostents of love
As shall conveniently become you there.'
And even there, his eye being big with tears,
Turning his face, he put his hand behind him,
And with affection wondrous sensible
He wrung Bassanio's hand; and so they parted.

SALANIO

I think he only loves the world for him.
I pray thee, let us go and find him out,
And quicken his embraced heaviness
With some delight or other.

SALARINO

Do we so.

Exeunt

SCENE IX. BELMONT. A ROOM IN PORTIA'S HOUSE

Enter NERISSA, with a SERVITOR

NERISSA

Quick, quick, I pray thee, draw the curtain straight;
The Prince of Arragon hath ta'en his oath,
And comes to his election presently.

Flourish of cornets. Enter the PRINCE OF
ARRAGON, PORTIA, and their Trains

PORTIA

    Behold, there stand the caskets, noble Prince:
    If you choose that wherein I am contain'd,
    Straight shall our nuptial rites be solemniz'd;
    But if you fail, without more speech, my lord,
    You must be gone from hence immediately.

ARRAGON

    I am enjoin'd by oath to observe three things:
    First, never to unfold to any one
    Which casket 'twas I chose; next, if I fail
    Of the right casket, never in my life
    To woo a maid in way of marriage;
    Lastly,
    If I do fail in fortune of my choice,
    Immediately to leave you and be gone.

PORTIA

    To these injunctions every one doth swear
    That comes to hazard for my worthless self.

ARRAGON

    And so have I address'd me. Fortune now
    To my heart's hope! Gold, silver, and base lead.
    'Who chooseth me must give and hazard all he
        hath.'
    You shall look fairer ere I give or hazard.
    What says the golden chest? Ha! let me see:

'Who chooseth me shall gain what many men
    desire.'
What many men desire! that 'many' may be
    meant
By the fool multitude, that choose by show,
Not learning more than the fond eye doth
    teach;
Which pries not to th' interior, but, like the
    martlet,
Builds in the weather on the outward wall,
Even in the force and road of casualty.
I will not choose what many men desire,
Because I will not jump with common spirits
And rank me with the barbarous multitudes.
Why, then to thee, thou silver treasure-house;
Tell me once more what title thou dost bear:
'Who chooseth me shall get as much as he
    deserves.'
And well said too; for who shall go about
To cozen fortune, and be honourable
Without the stamp of merit? Let none presume
To wear an undeserved dignity.
O! that estates, degrees, and offices
Were not deriv'd corruptly, and that clear honour
Were purchas'd by the merit of the wearer!
How many then should cover that stand bare!
How many be commanded that command!

How much low peasantry would then be glean'd
From the true seed of honour; and how much
    honour
Pick'd from the chaff and ruin of the times
To be new varnish'd! Well, but to my choice:
'Who chooseth me shall get as much as he
    deserves.'
I will assume desert. Give me a key for this,
And instantly unlock my fortunes here.
[*He opens the silver casket.*]

PORTIA

  [*Aside*] Too long a pause for that which you
  find there.

ARRAGON

  What's here? The portrait of a blinking idiot,
  Presenting me a schedule! I will read it.
  How much unlike art thou to Portia!
  How much unlike my hopes and my deservings!
  'Who chooseth me shall have as much as he
     deserves.'
  Did I deserve no more than a fool's head?
  Is that my prize? Are my deserts no better?

PORTIA

  To offend, and judge, are distinct offices,
  And of opposed natures.

ARRAGON

  What is here? [*Reads.*]

'The fire seven times tried this;
Seven times tried that judgment is
That did never choose amiss.
Some there be that shadows kiss;
Such have but a shadow's bliss;
There be fools alive, I wis,
Silver'd o'er, and so was this.
Take what wife you will to bed,
I will ever be your head:
So be gone; you are sped.'
Still more fool I shall appear
By the time I linger here;
With one fool's head I came to woo,
But I go away with two.
Sweet, adieu! I'll keep my oath,
Patiently to bear my wroth.

Exit ARRAGON with his train.

PORTIA

Thus hath the candle sing'd the moth.
O, these deliberate fools! When they do choose,
They have the wisdom by their wit to lose.

NERISSA

The ancient saying is no heresy:
'Hanging and wiving goes by destiny.'

PORTIA

Come, draw the curtain, Nerissa.

Enter a SERVANT

SERVANT

Where is my lady?

PORTIA

Here; what would my lord?

SERVANT

Madam, there is alighted at your gate

A young Venetian, one that comes before

To signify th' approaching of his lord;

From whom he bringeth sensible regreets;

To wit, besides commends and courteous breath,

Gifts of rich value. Yet I have not seen

So likely an ambassador of love.

A day in April never came so sweet,

To show how costly summer was at hand,

As this fore-spurrer comes before his lord.

PORTIA

No more, I pray thee; I am half afeard

Thou wilt say anon he is some kin to thee,

Thou spend'st such high-day wit in praising him.

Come, come, Nerissa, for I long to see

Quick Cupid's post that comes so mannerly.

NERISSA

Bassanio, lord Love, if thy will it be!

Exeunt

Act III

SCENE I. VENICE. A STREET

Enter SALANIO and SALARINO

SALANIO

    Now, what news on the Rialto?

SALARINO

    Why, yet it lives there unchecked that Antonio
hath a ship of rich lading wrack'd on the narrow
seas; the Goodwins, I think they call the place, a
very dangerous flat and fatal, where the carcasses
of many a tall ship lie buried, as they say, if my
gossip Report be an honest woman of her word.

SALANIO

    I would she were as lying a gossip in that as
ever knapped ginger or made her neighbours
believe she wept for the death of a third
husband. But it is true, without any slips of
prolixity or crossing the plain highway of talk,

that the good Antonio, the honest Antonio. O
that I had a title good enough to keep his name
company!—

SALARINO

Come, the full stop.

SALANIO

Ha! What sayest thou? Why, the end is, he hath
lost a ship.

SALARINO

I would it might prove the end of his losses.

SALANIO

Let me say 'amen' betimes, lest the devil cross
my prayer, for here he comes in the likeness
of a Jew.

Enter SHYLOCK

How now, Shylock! What news among the
merchants?

SHYLOCK

You knew, none so well, none so well as you, of
my daughter's flight.

SALARINO

That's certain; I, for my part, knew the tailor
that made the wings she flew withal.

SALANIO

And Shylock, for his own part, knew the bird
was fledged; and then it is the complexion of
them all to leave the dam.

SHYLOCK

She is damned for it.

SALARINO

That's certain, if the devil may be her judge.

SHYLOCK

My own flesh and blood to rebel!

SALANIO

Out upon it, old carrion! Rebels it at these years?

SHYLOCK

I say my daughter is my flesh and my blood.

SALARINO

There is more difference between thy flesh and
hers than between jet and ivory; more between
your bloods than there is between red wine
and Rhenish. But tell us, do you hear whether
Antonio have had any loss at sea or no?

SHYLOCK

There I have another bad match: a bankrupt,
a prodigal, who dare scarce show his head
on the Rialto; a beggar, that used to come so
smug upon the mart; let him look to his bond:
he was wont to call me usurer; let him look
to his bond: he was wont to lend money for a
Christian courtesy; let him look to his bond.

SALARINO

Why, I am sure, if he forfeit, thou wilt not take
his flesh: what's that good for?

SHYLOCK

To bait fish withal: if it will feed nothing else, it will feed my revenge. He hath disgrac'd me and hind'red me half a million; laugh'd at my losses, mock'd at my gains, scorned my nation, thwarted my bargains, cooled my friends, heated mine enemies. And what's his reason? I am a Jew. Hath not a Jew eyes? Hath not a Jew hands, organs, dimensions, senses, affections, passions, fed with the same food, hurt with the same weapons, subject to the same diseases, healed by the same means, warmed and cooled by the same winter and summer, as a Christian is? If you prick us, do we not bleed? If you tickle us, do we not laugh? If you poison us, do we not die? And if you wrong us, shall we not revenge? If we are like you in the rest, we will resemble you in that. If a Jew wrong a Christian, what is his humility? Revenge. If a Christian wrong a Jew, what should his sufferance be by Christian example? Why, revenge. The villainy you teach me I will execute; and it shall go hard but I will better the instruction.

Enter a Servant

SERVANT

Gentlemen, my master Antonio is at his house, and desires to speak with you both.

SALARINO

We have been up and down to seek him.

Enter TUBAL

SALANIO

Here comes another of the tribe: a third cannot be match'd, unless the devil himself turn Jew.

*Exeunt SALANIO,
SALARINO, and Servant*

SHYLOCK

How now, Tubal! what news from Genoa? Hast thou found my daughter?

TUBAL

I often came where I did hear of her, but cannot find her.

SHYLOCK

Why there, there, there, there! A diamond gone, cost me two thousand ducats in Frankfort! The curse never fell upon our nation till now; I never felt it till now. Two thousand ducats in that, and other precious, precious jewels. I would my daughter were dead at my foot, and the jewels in her ear; would she were hearsed at my foot, and the ducats in her coffin! No news of them? Why, so—and I know not what's spent in the search. Why, thou—loss upon loss! The thief gone with so much, and so much to find the thief; and no satisfaction, no revenge; nor no ill luck stirring but what lights on my shoulders; no sighs but of my breathing; no tears but of my shedding.

TUBAL

Yes, other men have ill luck too. Antonio, as I heard in Genoa—

SHYLOCK

What, what, what? Ill luck, ill luck?

TUBAL

Hath an argosy cast away, coming from Tripolis.

SHYLOCK

I thank God! I thank God! Is it true, is it true?

TUBAL

I spoke with some of the sailors that escaped the wrack.

SHYLOCK

I thank thee, good Tubal. Good news, good news! ha, ha!

Where? in Genoa?

TUBAL

Your daughter spent in Genoa, as I heard, one night, fourscore ducats.

SHYLOCK

Thou stick'st a dagger in me—I shall never see my gold again: fourscore ducats at a sitting! Fourscore ducats!

TUBAL

There came divers of Antonio's creditors in my company to Venice that swear he cannot choose but break.

SHYLOCK

I am very glad of it; I'll plague him, I'll torture him; I am glad of it.

TUBAL

One of them showed me a ring that he had of your daughter for a monkey.

SHYLOCK

Out upon her! Thou torturest me, Tubal: It was my turquoise; I had it of Leah when I was a bachelor; I would not have given it for a wilderness of monkeys.

TUBAL

But Antonio is certainly undone.

SHYLOCK

Nay, that's true; that's very true. Go, Tubal, fee me an officer; bespeak him a fortnight before. I will have the heart of him, if he forfeit; for, were he out of Venice, I can make what merchandise I will. Go, Tubal, and meet me at our synagogue; go, good Tubal; at our synagogue, Tubal.

Exeunt

SCENE II. BELMONT. A ROOM IN PORTIA'S HOUSE

Enter BASSANIO, PORTIA, GRATIANO, NERISSA, and Attendants

PORTIA

    I pray you tarry; pause a day or two
    Before you hazard; for, in choosing wrong,
    I lose your company; therefore forbear a while.
    There's something tells me, but it is not love,
    I would not lose you; and you know yourself
    Hate counsels not in such a quality.
    But lest you should not understand me well—
    And yet a maiden hath no tongue but thought—
    I would detain you here some month or two
    Before you venture for me. I could teach you
    How to choose right, but then I am forsworn;
    So will I never be; so may you miss me;
    But if you do, you'll make me wish a sin,
    That I had been forsworn. Beshrew your eyes!
    They have o'erlook'd me and divided me:
    One half of me is yours, the other half yours,
    Mine own, I would say; but if mine, then yours,
    And so all yours. O! these naughty times
    Puts bars between the owners and their rights;
    And so, though yours, not yours. Prove it so,
    Let fortune go to hell for it, not I.

I speak too long, but 'tis to peize the time,
To eke it, and to draw it out in length,
To stay you from election.

BASSANIO

Let me choose;
For as I am, I live upon the rack.

PORTIA

Upon the rack, Bassanio! Then confess
What treason there is mingled with your love.

BASSANIO

None but that ugly treason of mistrust,
Which makes me fear th' enjoying of my love:
There may as well be amity and life
'Tween snow and fire as treason and my love.

PORTIA

Ay, but I fear you speak upon the rack,
Where men enforced do speak anything.

BASSANIO

Promise me life, and I'll confess the truth.

PORTIA

Well then, confess and live.

BASSANIO

'Confess' and 'love'
Had been the very sum of my confession:
O happy torment, when my torturer
Doth teach me answers for deliverance!
But let me to my fortune and the caskets.

PORTIA

Away, then! I am lock'd in one of them:
If you do love me, you will find me out.
Nerissa and the rest, stand all aloof;
Let music sound while he doth make his choice;
Then, if he lose, he makes a swan-like end,
Fading in music: that the comparison
May stand more proper, my eye shall be the
    stream
And watery death-bed for him. He may win;
And what is music then? Then music is
Even as the flourish when true subjects bow
To a new-crowned monarch; such it is
As are those dulcet sounds in break of day
That creep into the dreaming bridegroom's ear
And summon him to marriage. Now he goes,
With no less presence, but with much more love,
Than young Alcides when he did redeem
The virgin tribute paid by howling Troy
To the sea-monster: I stand for sacrifice;
The rest aloof are the Dardanian wives,
With bleared visages come forth to view
The issue of th' exploit. Go, Hercules!
Live thou, I live. With much much more dismay
I view the fight than thou that mak'st the fray.
[*A Song, whilst BASSANIO comments on the caskets to himself.*]

84

Tell me where is fancy bred,
Or in the heart or in the head,
How begot, how nourished?
Reply, reply.
It is engend'red in the eyes,
With gazing fed; and fancy dies
In the cradle where it lies.
Let us all ring fancy's knell:
I'll begin it.—Ding, dong, bell.

ALL

Ding, dong, bell.

BASSANIO

So may the outward shows be least themselves:
The world is still deceiv'd with ornament.
In law, what plea so tainted and corrupt
But, being season'd with a gracious voice,
Obscures the show of evil? In religion,
What damned error but some sober brow
Will bless it, and approve it with a text,
Hiding the grossness with fair ornament?
There is no vice so simple but assumes
Some mark of virtue on his outward parts.
How many cowards, whose hearts are all as
false
As stairs of sand, wear yet upon their chins
The beards of Hercules and frowning Mars;
Who, inward search'd, have livers white as milk;

And these assume but valour's excrement
To render them redoubted! Look on beauty
And you shall see 'tis purchas'd by the weight:
Which therein works a miracle in nature,
Making them lightest that wear most of it:
So are those crisped snaky golden locks
Which make such wanton gambols with the
    wind,
Upon supposed fairness, often known
To be the dowry of a second head,
The skull that bred them, in the sepulchre.
Thus ornament is but the guiled shore
To a most dangerous sea; the beauteous scarf
Veiling an Indian beauty; in a word,
The seeming truth which cunning times put on
To entrap the wisest. Therefore, thou gaudy
    gold,
Hard food for Midas, I will none of thee;
Nor none of thee, thou pale and common
    drudge
'Tween man and man: but thou, thou meagre
    lead,
Which rather threaten'st than dost promise
    aught,
Thy plainness moves me more than eloquence,
And here choose I: joy be the consequence!

PORTIA

    [*Aside*] How all the other passions fleet to air,
    As doubtful thoughts, and rash-embrac'd despair,
    And shuddering fear, and green-ey'd jealousy!
    O love! be moderate; allay thy ecstasy;
    In measure rain thy joy; scant this excess;
    I feel too much thy blessing; make it less,
    For fear I surfeit!

BASSANIO

    What find I here? [*Opening the leaden casket.*]
    Fair Portia's counterfeit! What demi-god
    Hath come so near creation? Move these eyes?
    Or whether riding on the balls of mine,
    Seem they in motion? Here are sever'd lips,
    Parted with sugar breath; so sweet a bar
    Should sunder such sweet friends. Here in her
        hairs
    The painter plays the spider, and hath woven
    A golden mesh t' entrap the hearts of men
    Faster than gnats in cobwebs: but her eyes!—
    How could he see to do them? Having made
        one,
    Methinks it should have power to steal both his,
    And leave itself unfurnish'd: yet look, how far
    The substance of my praise doth wrong this
        shadow

In underprizing it, so far this shadow
Doth limp behind the substance. Here's the scroll,
The continent and summary of my fortune.
'You that choose not by the view,
Chance as fair and choose as true!
Since this fortune falls to you,
Be content and seek no new.
If you be well pleas'd with this,
And hold your fortune for your bliss,
Turn to where your lady is
And claim her with a loving kiss.'
A gentle scroll. Fair lady, by your leave; [*Kissing her.*]
I come by note, to give and to receive.
Like one of two contending in a prize,
That thinks he hath done well in people's eyes,
Hearing applause and universal shout,
Giddy in spirit, still gazing in a doubt
Whether those peals of praise be his or no;
So, thrice-fair lady, stand I, even so,
As doubtful whether what I see be true,
Until confirm'd, sign'd, ratified by you.

PORTIA

You see me, Lord Bassanio, where I stand,
Such as I am: though for myself alone
I would not be ambitious in my wish

To wish myself much better, yet for you
I would be trebled twenty times myself,
A thousand times more fair, ten thousand times
    more rich;
That only to stand high in your account,
I might in virtues, beauties, livings, friends,
Exceed account. But the full sum of me
Is sum of something which, to term in gross,
Is an unlesson'd girl, unschool'd, unpractis'd;
Happy in this, she is not yet so old
But she may learn; happier than this,
She is not bred so dull but she can learn;
Happiest of all is that her gentle spirit
Commits itself to yours to be directed,
As from her lord, her governor, her king.
Myself and what is mine to you and yours
Is now converted. But now I was the lord
Of this fair mansion, master of my servants,
Queen o'er myself; and even now, but now,
This house, these servants, and this same
    myself,
Are yours—my lord's. I give them with this ring,
Which when you part from, lose, or give away,
Let it presage the ruin of your love,
And be my vantage to exclaim on you.

BASSANIO

Madam, you have bereft me of all words,

Only my blood speaks to you in my veins;
And there is such confusion in my powers
As, after some oration fairly spoke
By a beloved prince, there doth appear
Among the buzzing pleased multitude;
Where every something, being blent together,
Turns to a wild of nothing, save of joy,
Express'd and not express'd. But when this ring
Parts from this finger, then parts life from
    hence:
    O! then be bold to say Bassanio's dead.

NERISSA

My lord and lady, it is now our time,
That have stood by and seen our wishes prosper,
To cry, 'Good joy'. Good joy, my lord and lady!

GRATIANO

My Lord Bassanio, and my gentle lady,
I wish you all the joy that you can wish;
For I am sure you can wish none from me;
And when your honours mean to solemnize
The bargain of your faith, I do beseech you
Even at that time I may be married too.

BASSANIO

With all my heart, so thou canst get a wife.

GRATIANO

I thank your lordship, you have got me one.
My eyes, my lord, can look as swift as yours:

You saw the mistress, I beheld the maid;
You lov'd, I lov'd; for intermission
No more pertains to me, my lord, than you.
Your fortune stood upon the caskets there,
And so did mine too, as the matter falls;
For wooing here until I sweat again,
And swearing till my very roof was dry
With oaths of love, at last, if promise last,
I got a promise of this fair one here
To have her love, provided that your fortune
Achiev'd her mistress.

PORTIA

Is this true, Nerissa?

NERISSA

Madam, it is, so you stand pleas'd withal.

BASSANIO

And do you, Gratiano, mean good faith?

GRATIANO

Yes, faith, my lord.

BASSANIO

Our feast shall be much honour'd in your
marriage.

GRATIANO

We'll play with them the first boy for a
thousand ducats.

NERISSA

What! and stake down?

GRATIANO

No; we shall ne'er win at that sport, and stake
    down.
But who comes here? Lorenzo and his infidel?
What, and my old Venetian friend, Salanio!

Enter LORENZO,
JESSICA, and SALANIO

BASSANIO

Lorenzo and Salanio, welcome hither,
If that the youth of my new interest here
Have power to bid you welcome. By your leave,
I bid my very friends and countrymen,
Sweet Portia, welcome.

PORTIA

So do I, my lord;
They are entirely welcome.

LORENZO

I thank your honour. For my part, my lord,
My purpose was not to have seen you here;
But meeting with Salanio by the way,
He did entreat me, past all saying nay,
To come with him along.

SALANIO

I did, my lord,
And I have reason for it. Signior Antonio
Commends him to you.

Gives BASSANIO a letter

BASSANIO

Ere I ope his letter,

I pray you tell me how my good friend doth.

SALANIO

Not sick, my lord, unless it be in mind;

Nor well, unless in mind; his letter there

Will show you his estate.

BASSANIO opens the letter

GRATIANO

Nerissa, cheer yon stranger; bid her welcome.

Your hand, Salanio. What's the news from Venice?

How doth that royal merchant, good Antonio?

I know he will be glad of our success:

We are the Jasons, we have won the fleece.

SALANIO

I would you had won the fleece that he hath lost.

PORTIA

There are some shrewd contents in yon same paper.

That steal the colour from Bassanio's cheek:

Some dear friend dead, else nothing in the world

Could turn so much the constitution

Of any constant man. What, worse and worse!

With leave, Bassanio: I am half yourself,

And I must freely have the half of anything
That this same paper brings you.

BASSANIO

O sweet Portia!
Here are a few of the unpleasant'st words
That ever blotted paper. Gentle lady,
When I did first impart my love to you,
I freely told you all the wealth I had
Ran in my veins, I was a gentleman;
And then I told you true. And yet, dear lady,
Rating myself at nothing, you shall see
How much I was a braggart. When I told you
My state was nothing, I should then have told
    you
That I was worse than nothing; for indeed
I have engag'd myself to a dear friend,
Engag'd my friend to his mere enemy,
To feed my means. Here is a letter, lady,
The paper as the body of my friend,
And every word in it a gaping wound
Issuing life-blood. But is it true, Salanio?
Hath all his ventures fail'd? What, not one hit?
From Tripolis, from Mexico, and England,
From Lisbon, Barbary, and India?
And not one vessel scape the dreadful touch
Of merchant-marring rocks?

SALANIO

Not one, my lord.
Besides, it should appear that, if he had
The present money to discharge the Jew,
He would not take it. Never did I know
A creature that did bear the shape of man,
So keen and greedy to confound a man.
He plies the Duke at morning and at night,
And doth impeach the freedom of the state,
If they deny him justice. Twenty merchants,
The Duke himself, and the magnificoes
Of greatest port, have all persuaded with him;
But none can drive him from the envious plea
Of forfeiture, of justice, and his bond.

JESSICA

When I was with him, I have heard him swear
To Tubal and to Chus, his countrymen,
That he would rather have Antonio's flesh
Than twenty times the value of the sum
That he did owe him; and I know, my lord,
If law, authority, and power, deny not,
It will go hard with poor Antonio.

PORTIA

Is it your dear friend that is thus in trouble?

BASSANIO

The dearest friend to me, the kindest man,

The best condition'd and unwearied spirit
In doing courtesies; and one in whom
The ancient Roman honour more appears
Than any that draws breath in Italy.

PORTIA

What sum owes he the Jew?

BASSANIO

For me, three thousand ducats.

PORTIA

What! no more?
Pay him six thousand, and deface the bond;
Double six thousand, and then treble that,
Before a friend of this description
Shall lose a hair through Bassanio's fault.
First go with me to church and call me wife,
And then away to Venice to your friend;
For never shall you lie by Portia's side
With an unquiet soul. You shall have gold
To pay the petty debt twenty times over:
When it is paid, bring your true friend along.
My maid Nerissa and myself meantime,
Will live as maids and widows. Come, away!
For you shall hence upon your wedding day.
Bid your friends welcome, show a merry cheer;
Since you are dear bought, I will love you dear.
But let me hear the letter of your friend.

BASSANIO

> [*Reads*] 'Sweet Bassanio, my ships have all
> miscarried, my creditors grow cruel, my estate
> is very low, my bond to the Jew is forfeit; and
> since, in paying it, it is impossible I should live,
> all debts are clear'd between you and I, if I might
> but see you at my death. Notwithstanding, use
> your pleasure; if your love do not persuade you
> to come, let not my letter.'

PORTIA

> O love, dispatch all business and be gone!

BASSANIO

> Since I have your good leave to go away,
> I will make haste; but, till I come again,
> No bed shall e'er be guilty of my stay,
> Nor rest be interposer 'twixt us twain.

> > > > > > > *Exeunt*

SCENE III. VENICE. A STREET

*Enter SHYLOCK, SALARINO, ANTONIO, and
Gaoler*

SHYLOCK

> Gaoler, look to him. Tell not me of mercy;
> This is the fool that lent out money gratis:
> Gaoler, look to him.

ANTONIO

Hear me yet, good Shylock.

SHYLOCK

I'll have my bond; speak not against my bond.
I have sworn an oath that I will have my bond.
Thou call'dst me dog before thou hadst a cause,
But, since I am a dog, beware my fangs;
The Duke shall grant me justice. I do wonder,
Thou naughty gaoler, that thou art so fond
To come abroad with him at his request.

ANTONIO

I pray thee hear me speak.

SHYLOCK

I'll have my bond. I will not hear thee speak;
I'll have my bond; and therefore speak no more.
I'll not be made a soft and dull-eyed fool,
To shake the head, relent, and sigh, and yield
To Christian intercessors. Follow not;
I'll have no speaking; I will have my bond.

Exit

SALARINO

It is the most impenetrable cur
That ever kept with men.

ANTONIO

Let him alone;
I'll follow him no more with bootless prayers.
He seeks my life; his reason well I know:

I oft deliver'd from his forfeitures
Many that have at times made moan to me;
Therefore he hates me.

SALARINO

I am sure the Duke
Will never grant this forfeiture to hold.

ANTONIO

The Duke cannot deny the course of law;
For the commodity that strangers have
With us in Venice, if it be denied,
'Twill much impeach the justice of the state,
Since that the trade and profit of the city
Consisteth of all nations. Therefore, go;
These griefs and losses have so bated me
That I shall hardly spare a pound of flesh
To-morrow to my bloody creditor.
Well, gaoler, on; pray God Bassanio come
To see me pay his debt, and then I care not.

Exeunt

SCENE IV. BELMONT. A ROOM IN PORTIA'S HOUSE

Enter PORTIA, NERISSA, LORENZO, JESSICA, and BALTHASAR

LORENZO

    Madam, although I speak it in your presence,

    You have a noble and a true conceit

    Of godlike amity, which appears most strongly

    In bearing thus the absence of your lord.

    But if you knew to whom you show this honour,

    How true a gentleman you send relief,

    How dear a lover of my lord your husband,

    I know you would be prouder of the work

    Than customary bounty can enforce you.

PORTIA

    I never did repent for doing good,

    Nor shall not now; for in companions

    That do converse and waste the time together,

    Whose souls do bear an equal yoke of love,

    There must be needs a like proportion

    Of lineaments, of manners, and of spirit,

    Which makes me think that this Antonio,

    Being the bosom lover of my lord,

    Must needs be like my lord. If it be so,

    How little is the cost I have bestowed

    In purchasing the semblance of my soul

From out the state of hellish cruelty!
This comes too near the praising of myself;
Therefore, no more of it; hear other things.
Lorenzo, I commit into your hands
The husbandry and manage of my house
Until my lord's return; for mine own part,
I have toward heaven breath'd a secret vow
To live in prayer and contemplation,
Only attended by Nerissa here,
Until her husband and my lord's return.
There is a monastery two miles off,
And there we will abide. I do desire you
Not to deny this imposition,
The which my love and some necessity
Now lays upon you.

LORENZO

Madam, with all my heart
I shall obey you in all fair commands.

PORTIA

My people do already know my mind,
And will acknowledge you and Jessica
In place of Lord Bassanio and myself.
So fare you well till we shall meet again.

LORENZO

Fair thoughts and happy hours attend on you!

JESSICA

I wish your ladyship all heart's content.

PORTIA

> I thank you for your wish, and am well pleas'd
> To wish it back on you. Fare you well, Jessica.

Exeunt JESSICA and
LORENZO

> Now, Balthasar,
> As I have ever found thee honest-true,
> So let me find thee still. Take this same letter,
> And use thou all th' endeavour of a man
> In speed to Padua; see thou render this
> Into my cousin's hands, Doctor Bellario;
> And look what notes and garments he doth
>   give thee,
> Bring them, I pray thee, with imagin'd speed
> Unto the traject, to the common ferry
> Which trades to Venice. Waste no time in words,
> But get thee gone; I shall be there before thee.

BALTHASAR

> Madam, I go with all convenient speed.

Exit

PORTIA

> Come on, Nerissa, I have work in hand
> That you yet know not of; we'll see our husbands
> Before they think of us.

NERISSA

> Shall they see us?

PORTIA

 They shall, Nerissa; but in such a habit
 That they shall think we are accomplished
 With that we lack. I'll hold thee any wager,
 When we are both accoutred like young men,
 I'll prove the prettier fellow of the two,
 And wear my dagger with the braver grace,
 And speak between the change of man and boy
 With a reed voice; and turn two mincing steps
 Into a manly stride; and speak of frays
 Like a fine bragging youth; and tell quaint lies,
 How honourable ladies sought my love,
 Which I denying, they fell sick and died;
 I could not do withal. Then I'll repent,
 And wish for all that, that I had not kill'd them.
 And twenty of these puny lies I'll tell,
 That men shall swear I have discontinu'd school
 About a twelvemonth. I have within my mind
 A thousand raw tricks of these bragging Jacks,
 Which I will practise.

NERISSA

 Why, shall we turn to men?

PORTIA

 Fie, what a question's that,
 If thou wert near a lewd interpreter!
 But come, I'll tell thee all my whole device

When I am in my coach, which stays for us
At the park gate; and therefore haste away,
For we must measure twenty miles to-day.

Exeunt

SCENE V. BELMONT. A GARDEN

Enter LAUNCELOT and JESSICA

LAUNCELOT

Yes, truly; for, look you, the sins of the father
are to be laid upon the children; therefore, I
promise you, I fear you. I was always plain with
you, and so now I speak my agitation of the
matter; therefore be of good cheer, for truly I
think you are damn'd. There is but one hope in
it that can do you any good, and that is but a
kind of bastard hope neither.

JESSICA

And what hope is that, I pray thee?

LAUNCELOT

Marry, you may partly hope that your father
got you not, that you are not the Jew's daughter.

JESSICA

That were a kind of bastard hope indeed; so the
sins of my mother should be visited upon me.

LAUNCELOT

Truly then I fear you are damn'd both by father

and mother; thus when I shun Scylla, your
father, I fall into Charybdis, your mother; well,
you are gone both ways.

JESSICA

I shall be saved by my husband; he hath made
me a Christian.

LAUNCELOT

Truly, the more to blame he; we were Christians
enow before, e'en as many as could well live
one by another. This making of Christians
will raise the price of hogs; if we grow all to be
pork-eaters, we shall not shortly have a rasher
on the coals for money.

JESSICA

I'll tell my husband, Launcelot, what you say;
here he comes.

Enter LORENZO

LORENZO

I shall grow jealous of you shortly, Launcelot,
if you thus get my wife into corners.

JESSICA

Nay, you need nor fear us, Lorenzo; Launcelot
and I are out; he tells me flatly there's no
mercy for me in heaven, because I am a Jew's
daughter; and he says you are no good member
of the commonwealth, for in converting Jews
to Christians you raise the price of pork.

LORENZO

I shall answer that better to the commonwealth than you can the getting up of the negro's belly; the Moor is with child by you, Launcelot.

LAUNCELOT

It is much that the Moor should be more than reason; but if she be less than an honest woman, she is indeed more than I took her for.

LORENZO

How every fool can play upon the word! I think the best grace of wit will shortly turn into silence, and discourse grow commendable in none only but parrots. Go in, sirrah; bid them prepare for dinner.

LAUNCELOT

That is done, sir; they have all stomachs.

LORENZO

Goodly Lord, what a wit-snapper are you! Then bid them prepare dinner.

LAUNCELOT

That is done too, sir, only 'cover' is the word.

LORENZO

Will you cover, then, sir?

LAUNCELOT

Not so, sir, neither; I know my duty.

LORENZO

Yet more quarrelling with occasion! Wilt thou

show the whole wealth of thy wit in an instant?
I pray thee understand a plain man in his plain
meaning: go to thy fellows, bid them cover the
table, serve in the meat, and we will come in
to dinner.

LAUNCELOT

For the table, sir, it shall be served in; for the
meat, sir, it shall be covered; for your coming
in to dinner, sir, why, let it be as humours and
conceits shall govern.

Exit

LORENZO

O dear discretion, how his words are suited!
The fool hath planted in his memory
An army of good words; and I do know
A many fools that stand in better place,
Garnish'd like him, that for a tricksy word
Defy the matter. How cheer'st thou, Jessica?
And now, good sweet, say thy opinion,
How dost thou like the Lord Bassanio's wife?

JESSICA

Past all expressing. It is very meet
The Lord Bassanio live an upright life,
For, having such a blessing in his lady,
He finds the joys of heaven here on earth;
And if on earth he do not merit it,
In reason he should never come to heaven.

Why, if two gods should play some heavenly
match,
And on the wager lay two earthly women,
And Portia one, there must be something else
Pawn'd with the other; for the poor rude world
Hath not her fellow.

LORENZO

Even such a husband
Hast thou of me as she is for a wife.

JESSICA

Nay, but ask my opinion too of that.

LORENZO

I will anon; first let us go to dinner.

JESSICA

Nay, let me praise you while I have a stomach.

LORENZO

No, pray thee, let it serve for table-talk;
Then howsoe'er thou speak'st, 'mong other
things
I shall digest it.

JESSICA

Well, I'll set you forth.

Exeunt

Act IV

SCENE I. VENICE. A COURT OF JUSTICE

Enter the DUKE: the Magnificoes; ANTONIO,
BASSANIO, GRATIANO, SALARINO,
SALANIO, and Others

DUKE
    What, is Antonio here?

ANTONIO
    Ready, so please your Grace.

DUKE
    I am sorry for thee; thou art come to answer
    A stony adversary, an inhuman wretch,
    Uncapable of pity, void and empty
    From any dram of mercy.

ANTONIO
    I have heard
    Your Grace hath ta'en great pains to qualify

His rigorous course; but since he stands obdurate,
And that no lawful means can carry me
Out of his envy's reach, I do oppose
My patience to his fury, and am arm'd
To suffer with a quietness of spirit
The very tyranny and rage of his.

DUKE

Go one, and call the Jew into the court.

SALARINO

He is ready at the door; he comes, my lord.

Enter SHYLOCK

DUKE

Make room, and let him stand before our face.
Shylock, the world thinks, and I think so too,
That thou but leadest this fashion of thy malice
To the last hour of act; and then, 'tis thought,
Thou'lt show thy mercy and remorse, more strange
Than is thy strange apparent cruelty;
And where thou now exacts the penalty,
Which is a pound of this poor merchant's flesh,
Thou wilt not only loose the forfeiture,
But, touch'd with human gentleness and love,
Forgive a moiety of the principal,
Glancing an eye of pity on his losses,
That have of late so huddled on his back,

Enow to press a royal merchant down,
And pluck commiseration of his state
From brassy bosoms and rough hearts of flint,
From stubborn Turks and Tartars, never train'd
To offices of tender courtesy.
We all expect a gentle answer, Jew.

SHYLOCK

I have possess'd your Grace of what I purpose,
And by our holy Sabbath have I sworn
To have the due and forfeit of my bond.
If you deny it, let the danger light
Upon your charter and your city's freedom.
You'll ask me why I rather choose to have
A weight of carrion flesh than to receive
Three thousand ducats. I'll not answer that,
But say it is my humour: is it answer'd?
What if my house be troubled with a rat,
And I be pleas'd to give ten thousand ducats
To have it ban'd? What, are you answer'd yet?
Some men there are love not a gaping pig;
Some that are mad if they behold a cat;
And others, when the bagpipe sings i' the nose,
Cannot contain their urine; for affection,
Mistress of passion, sways it to the mood
Of what it likes or loathes. Now, for your
      answer:
As there is no firm reason to be render'd,

Why he cannot abide a gaping pig;
Why he, a harmless necessary cat;
Why he, a wauling bagpipe; but of force
Must yield to such inevitable shame
As to offend, himself being offended;
So can I give no reason, nor I will not,
More than a lodg'd hate and a certain loathing
I bear Antonio, that I follow thus
A losing suit against him. Are you answered?

BASSANIO

This is no answer, thou unfeeling man,
To excuse the current of thy cruelty.

SHYLOCK

I am not bound to please thee with my answer.

BASSANIO

Do all men kill the things they do not love?

SHYLOCK

Hates any man the thing he would not kill?

BASSANIO

Every offence is not a hate at first.

SHYLOCK

What! wouldst thou have a serpent sting thee
twice?

ANTONIO

I pray you, think you question with the Jew.
You may as well go stand upon the beach,
And bid the main flood bate his usual height;

You may as well use question with the wolf,
Why he hath made the ewe bleat for the lamb;
You may as well forbid the mountain pines
To wag their high tops and to make no noise
When they are fretten with the gusts of heaven;
You may as well do anything most hard
As seek to soften that—than which what's
    harder?—
His Jewish heart: therefore, I do beseech you,
Make no moe offers, use no farther means,
But with all brief and plain conveniency.
Let me have judgment, and the Jew his will.

BASSANIO

For thy three thousand ducats here is six.

SHYLOCK

If every ducat in six thousand ducats
Were in six parts, and every part a ducat,
I would not draw them; I would have my bond.

DUKE

How shalt thou hope for mercy, rendering
none?

SHYLOCK

What judgment shall I dread, doing no wrong?
You have among you many a purchas'd slave,
Which, like your asses and your dogs and mules,
You use in abject and in slavish parts,
Because you bought them; shall I say to you

'Let them be free, marry them to your heirs—
Why sweat they under burdens?—let their beds
Be made as soft as yours, and let their palates
Be season'd with such viands'? You will answer
'The slaves are ours.' So do I answer you:
The pound of flesh which I demand of him
Is dearly bought; 'tis mine, and I will have it.
If you deny me, fie upon your law!
There is no force in the decrees of Venice.
I stand for judgment: answer; shall I have it?

DUKE

Upon my power I may dismiss this court,
Unless Bellario, a learned doctor,
Whom I have sent for to determine this,
Come here to-day.

SALARINO

My lord, here stays without
A messenger with letters from the doctor,
New come from Padua.

DUKE

Bring us the letters; call the messenger.

BASSANIO

Good cheer, Antonio! What, man, courage yet!
The Jew shall have my flesh, blood, bones, and
    all,
Ere thou shalt lose for me one drop of blood.

ANTONIO

I am a tainted wether of the flock,
Meetest for death; the weakest kind of fruit
Drops earliest to the ground, and so let me.
You cannot better be employ'd, Bassanio,
Than to live still, and write mine epitaph.

*Enter NERISSA dressed
like a lawyer's clerk.*

DUKE

Came you from Padua, from Bellario?

NERISSA

From both, my lord. Bellario greets your
Grace.

[*Presents a letter.*]

BASSANIO

Why dost thou whet thy knife so earnestly?

SHYLOCK

To cut the forfeiture from that bankrupt there.

GRATIANO

Not on thy sole, but on thy soul, harsh Jew,
Thou mak'st thy knife keen; but no metal can,
No, not the hangman's axe, bear half the
keenness
Of thy sharp envy. Can no prayers pierce thee?

SHYLOCK

No, none that thou hast wit enough to make.

GRATIANO

O, be thou damn'd, inexecrable dog!
And for thy life let justice be accus'd.
Thou almost mak'st me waver in my faith,
To hold opinion with Pythagoras
That souls of animals infuse themselves
Into the trunks of men. Thy currish spirit
Govern'd a wolf who, hang'd for human slaughter,
Even from the gallows did his fell soul fleet,
And, whilst thou lay'st in thy unhallow'd dam,
Infus'd itself in thee; for thy desires
Are wolfish, bloody, starv'd and ravenous.

SHYLOCK

Till thou canst rail the seal from off my bond,
Thou but offend'st thy lungs to speak so loud;
Repair thy wit, good youth, or it will fall
To cureless ruin. I stand here for law.

DUKE

This letter from Bellario doth commend
A young and learned doctor to our court.
Where is he?

NERISSA

He attendeth here hard by,
To know your answer, whether you'll admit him.

DUKE OF VENICE

With all my heart: some three or four of you

116

Go give him courteous conduct to this place.
Meantime, the court shall hear Bellario's letter.

CLERK

[*Reads*] 'Your Grace shall understand that at
the receipt of your letter I am very sick; but in
the instant that your messenger came, in loving
visitation was with me a young doctor of Rome;
his name is Balthazar. I acquainted him with
the cause in controversy between the Jew and
Antonio the merchant; we turn'd o'er many
books together; he is furnished with my opinion
which, bettered with his own learning—the
greatness whereof I cannot enough commend—
comes with him at my importunity to fill up
your Grace's request in my stead. I beseech you
let his lack of years be no impediment to let him
lack a reverend estimation, for I never knew so
young a body with so old a head. I leave him
to your gracious acceptance, whose trial shall
better publish his commendation.'

DUKE

YOU hear the learn'd Bellario, what he writes;
And here, I take it, is the doctor come.

*Enter PORTIA, dressed
like a doctor of laws.*

Give me your hand; come you from old
Bellario?

117

PORTIA

    I did, my lord.

DUKE

    You are welcome; take your place.

    Are you acquainted with the difference

    That holds this present question in the court?

PORTIA

    I am informed throughly of the cause.

    Which is the merchant here, and which the Jew?

DUKE OF VENICE

    Antonio and old Shylock, both stand forth.

PORTIA

    Is your name Shylock?

SHYLOCK

    Shylock is my name.

PORTIA

    Of a strange nature is the suit you follow;

    Yet in such rule that the Venetian law

    Cannot impugn you as you do proceed.

    [*To ANTONIO.*] You stand within his danger,

        do you not?

ANTONIO

    Ay, so he says.

PORTIA

    Do you confess the bond?

ANTONIO

    I do.

PORTIA

Then must the Jew be merciful.

SHYLOCK

On what compulsion must I? Tell me that.

PORTIA

The quality of mercy is not strain'd;
It droppeth as the gentle rain from heaven
Upon the place beneath. It is twice blest:
It blesseth him that gives and him that takes.
'Tis mightiest in the mightiest; it becomes
The throned monarch better than his crown;
His sceptre shows the force of temporal power,
The attribute to awe and majesty,
Wherein doth sit the dread and fear of kings;
But mercy is above this sceptred sway,
It is enthroned in the hearts of kings,
It is an attribute to God himself;
And earthly power doth then show likest
    God's
When mercy seasons justice. Therefore, Jew,
Though justice be thy plea, consider this,
That in the course of justice none of us
Should see salvation; we do pray for mercy,
And that same prayer doth teach us all to render
The deeds of mercy. I have spoke thus much
To mitigate the justice of thy plea,
Which if thou follow, this strict court of Venice

Must needs give sentence 'gainst the merchant
    there.

SHYLOCK

    My deeds upon my head! I crave the law,
    The penalty and forfeit of my bond.

PORTIA

    Is he not able to discharge the money?

BASSANIO

    Yes; here I tender it for him in the court;
    Yea, twice the sum; if that will not suffice,
    I will be bound to pay it ten times o'er
    On forfeit of my hands, my head, my heart;
    If this will not suffice, it must appear
    That malice bears down truth. And, I beseech
      you,
    Wrest once the law to your authority;
    To do a great right do a little wrong,
    And curb this cruel devil of his will.

PORTIA

    It must not be; there is no power in Venice
    Can alter a decree established;
    'Twill be recorded for a precedent,
    And many an error by the same example
    Will rush into the state. It cannot be.

SHYLOCK

    A Daniel come to judgment! Yea, a Daniel!
    O wise young judge, how I do honour thee!

PORTIA

I pray you, let me look upon the bond.

SHYLOCK

Here 'tis, most reverend doctor; here it is.

PORTIA

Shylock, there's thrice thy money offer'd thee.

SHYLOCK

An oath, an oath! I have an oath in heaven.

Shall I lay perjury upon my soul?

No, not for Venice.

PORTIA

Why, this bond is forfeit;

And lawfully by this the Jew may claim

A pound of flesh, to be by him cut off

Nearest the merchant's heart. Be merciful.

Take thrice thy money; bid me tear the bond.

SHYLOCK

When it is paid according to the tenour.

It doth appear you are a worthy judge;

You know the law; your exposition

Hath been most sound; I charge you by the
law,

Whereof you are a well-descrving pillar,

Proceed to judgment. By my soul I swear

There is no power in the tongue of man

To alter me. I stay here on my bond.

ANTONIO

Most heartily I do beseech the court

To give the judgment.

PORTIA

Why then, thus it is:

You must prepare your bosom for his knife.

SHYLOCK

O noble judge! O excellent young man!

PORTIA

For the intent and purpose of the law

Hath full relation to the penalty,

Which here appeareth due upon the bond.

SHYLOCK

'Tis very true. O wise and upright judge,

How much more elder art thou than thy looks!

PORTIA

Therefore, lay bare your bosom.

SHYLOCK

Ay, his breast—

So says the bond; doth it not, noble judge?

'Nearest his heart', those are the very words.

PORTIA

It is so. Are there balance here to weigh

The flesh?

SHYLOCK

I have them ready.

PORTIA

Have by some surgeon, Shylock, on your charge,

To stop his wounds, lest he do bleed to death.

SHYLOCK

Is it so nominated in the bond?

PORTIA

It is not so express'd; but what of that?

'Twere good you do so much for charity.

SHYLOCK

I cannot find it; 'tis not in the bond.

PORTIA

You, merchant, have you anything to say?

ANTONIO

But little: I am arm'd and well prepar'd.

Give me your hand, Bassanio: fare you well.!

Grieve not that I am fallen to this for you,

For herein Fortune shows herself more kind

Than is her custom: it is still her use

To let the wretched man outlive his wealth,

To view with hollow eye and wrinkled brow

An age of poverty; from which lingering
    penance

Of such misery doth she cut me off.

Commend me to your honourable wife:

Tell her the process of Antonio's end;

Say how I lov'd you; speak me fair in death;

And, when the tale is told, bid her be judge
Whether Bassanio had not once a love.
Repent but you that you shall lose your friend,
And he repents not that he pays your debt;
For if the Jew do cut but deep enough,
I'll pay it instantly with all my heart.

BASSANIO

Antonio, I am married to a wife
Which is as dear to me as life itself;
But life itself, my wife, and all the world,
Are not with me esteem'd above thy life;
I would lose all, ay, sacrifice them all
Here to this devil, to deliver you.

PORTIA

Your wife would give you little thanks for that,
If she were by to hear you make the offer.

GRATIANO

I have a wife whom, I protest, I love;
I would she were in heaven, so she could
Entreat some power to change this currish Jew.

NERISSA

'Tis well you offer it behind her back;
The wish would make else an unquiet house.

SHYLOCK

[*Aside*] These be the Christian husbands! I have
    a daughter;
Would any of the stock of Barabbas

Had been her husband, rather than a Christian!
We trifle time; I pray thee, pursue sentence.

PORTIA

A pound of that same merchant's flesh is thine.
The court awards it and the law doth give it.

SHYLOCK

Most rightful judge!

PORTIA

And you must cut this flesh from off his breast.
The law allows it and the court awards it.

SHYLOCK

Most learned judge! A sentence! Come, prepare.

PORTIA

Tarry a little; there is something else.
This bond doth give thee here no jot of blood;
The words expressly are 'a pound of flesh':
Take then thy bond, take thou thy pound of
flesh;
But, in the cutting it, if thou dost shed
One drop of Christian blood, thy lands and
goods
Are, by the laws of Venice, confiscate
Unto the state of Venice.

GRATIANO

O upright judge! Mark, Jew: O learned judge!

SHYLOCK

Is that the law?

PORTIA

    Thyself shalt see the act;

    For, as thou urgest justice, be assur'd

    Thou shalt have justice, more than thou desir'st.

GRATIANO

    O learned judge! Mark, Jew: a learned judge!

SHYLOCK

    I take this offer then: pay the bond thrice,

    And let the Christian go.

BASSANIO

    Here is the money.

PORTIA

    Soft!

    The Jew shall have all justice. Soft! No haste.

    He shall have nothing but the penalty.

GRATIANO

    O Jew! an upright judge, a learned judge!

PORTIA

    Therefore, prepare thee to cut off the flesh.

    Shed thou no blood; nor cut thou less nor more,

    But just a pound of flesh: if thou tak'st more,

    Or less, than a just pound, be it but so much

    As makes it light or heavy in the substance,

    Or the division of the twentieth part

    Of one poor scruple; nay, if the scale do turn

    But in the estimation of a hair,

    Thou diest, and all thy goods are confiscate.

GRATIANO

A second Daniel, a Daniel, Jew!

Now, infidel, I have you on the hip.

PORTIA

Why doth the Jew pause? Take thy forfeiture.

SHYLOCK

Give me my principal, and let me go.

BASSANIO

I have it ready for thee; here it is.

PORTIA

He hath refus'd it in the open court;

He shall have merely justice, and his bond.

GRATIANO

A Daniel still say I; a second Daniel!

I thank thee, Jew, for teaching me that word.

SHYLOCK

Shall I not have barely my principal?

PORTIA

Thou shalt have nothing but the forfeiture

To be so taken at thy peril, Jew.

SHYLOCK

Why, then the devil give him good of it!

I'll stay no longer question.

PORTIA

Tarry, Jew.

The law hath yet another hold on you.

It is enacted in the laws of Venice,

If it be prov'd against an alien
That by direct or indirect attempts
He seek the life of any citizen,
The party 'gainst the which he doth contrive
Shall seize one half his goods; the other half
Comes to the privy coffer of the state;
And the offender's life lies in the mercy
Of the Duke only, 'gainst all other voice.
In which predicament, I say, thou stand'st;
For it appears by manifest proceeding
That indirectly, and directly too,
Thou hast contrived against the very life
Of the defendant; and thou hast incurr'd
The danger formerly by me rehears'd.
Down, therefore, and beg mercy of the Duke.

GRATIANO

Beg that thou mayst have leave to hang thyself;
And yet, thy wealth being forfeit to the state,
Thou hast not left the value of a cord;
Therefore thou must be hang'd at the state's
    charge.

DUKE

That thou shalt see the difference of our spirits,
I pardon thee thy life before thou ask it.
For half thy wealth, it is Antonio's;
The other half comes to the general state,
Which humbleness may drive unto a fine.

PORTIA

Ay, for the state; not for Antonio.

SHYLOCK

Nay, take my life and all, pardon not that:
You take my house when you do take the prop
That doth sustain my house; you take my life
When you do take the means whereby I live.

PORTIA

What mercy can you render him, Antonio?

GRATIANO

A halter gratis; nothing else, for God's sake!

ANTONIO

So please my lord the Duke and all the court
To quit the fine for one half of his goods;
I am content, so he will let me have
The other half in use, to render it
Upon his death unto the gentleman
That lately stole his daughter:
Two things provided more, that, for this
 favour,
He presently become a Christian;
The other, that he do record a gift,
Here in the court, of all he dies possess'd
Unto his son Lorenzo and his daughter.

DUKE

He shall do this, or else I do recant
The pardon that I late pronounced here.

PORTIA

Art thou contented, Jew? What dost thou say?

SHYLOCK

I am content.

PORTIA

Clerk, draw a deed of gift.

SHYLOCK

I pray you, give me leave to go from hence;
I am not well; send the deed after me
And I will sign it.

DUKE

Get thee gone, but do it.

GRATIANO

In christening shalt thou have two god-fathers;
Had I been judge, thou shouldst have had ten
    more,
To bring thee to the gallows, not to the font.

Exit SHYLOCK

DUKE

Sir, I entreat you home with me to dinner.

PORTIA

I humbly do desire your Grace of pardon;
I must away this night toward Padua,
And it is meet I presently set forth.

DUKE

I am sorry that your leisure serves you not.
Antonio, gratify this gentleman,

For in my mind you are much bound to him.

Exeunt DUKE,
Magnificoes, and Train

BASSANIO

Most worthy gentleman, I and my friend
Have by your wisdom been this day acquitted
Of grievous penalties; in lieu whereof
Three thousand ducats, due unto the Jew,
We freely cope your courteous pains withal.

ANTONIO

And stand indebted, over and above,
In love and service to you evermore.

PORTIA

He is well paid that is well satisfied;
And I, delivering you, am satisfied,
And therein do account myself well paid:
My mind was never yet more mercenary.
I pray you, know me when we meet again:
I wish you well, and so I take my leave.

BASSANIO

Dear sir, of force I must attempt you further;
Take some remembrance of us, as a tribute,
Not as fee. Grant me two things, I pray you,
Not to deny me, and to pardon me.

PORTIA

You press me far, and therefore I will yield.
[*To ANTONIO*]

Give me your gloves, I'll wear them for your sake.
[*To BASSANIO*]

And, for your love, I'll take this ring from you.
Do not draw back your hand; I'll take no more;
And you in love shall not deny me this.

BASSANIO

This ring, good sir? alas, it is a trifle;
I will not shame myself to give you this.

PORTIA

I will have nothing else but only this;
And now, methinks, I have a mind to it.

BASSANIO

There's more depends on this than on the value.
The dearest ring in Venice will I give you,
And find it out by proclamation:
Only for this, I pray you, pardon me.

PORTIA

I see, sir, you are liberal in offers;
You taught me first to beg, and now methinks
You teach me how a beggar should be answer'd.

BASSANIO

Good sir, this ring was given me by my wife;
And, when she put it on, she made me vow
That I should neither sell, nor give, nor lose it.

PORTIA

That 'scuse serves many men to save their gifts.
And if your wife be not a mad woman,

And know how well I have deserv'd this ring,
She would not hold out enemy for ever
For giving it to me. Well, peace be with you!
Exeunt PORTIA and NERISSA

ANTONIO
My Lord Bassanio, let him have the ring:
Let his deservings, and my love withal,
Be valued 'gainst your wife's commandment.

BASSANIO
Go, Gratiano, run and overtake him;
Give him the ring, and bring him, if thou canst,
Unto Antonio's house. Away! make haste.
Exit GRATIANO

Come, you and I will thither presently;
And in the morning early will we both
Fly toward Belmont. Come, Antonio.
Exeunt

SCENE II. VENICE. A STREET

Enter PORTIA and NERISSA
PORTIA
Inquire the Jew's house out, give him this deed,
And let him sign it; we'll away to-night,
And be a day before our husbands home.
This deed will be well welcome to Lorenzo.
Enter GRATIANO

GRATIANO

Fair sir, you are well o'erta'en.

My Lord Bassanio, upon more advice,

Hath sent you here this ring, and doth entreat

Your company at dinner.

PORTIA

That cannot be:

His ring I do accept most thankfully;

And so, I pray you, tell him: furthermore,

I pray you show my youth old Shylock's house.

GRATIANO

That will I do.

NERISSA

Sir, I would speak with you.

[*Aside to PORTIA.*]

I'll see if I can get my husband's ring,

Which I did make him swear to keep for ever.

PORTIA

[*To NERISSA*]

Thou mayst, I warrant. We shall have old
    swearing

That they did give the rings away to men;

But we'll outface them, and outswear them too.

Away! make haste: thou know'st where I will tarry.

NERISSA

Come, good sir, will you show me to this house?

Exeunt

Act V

SCENE I. BELMONT. THE AVENUE TO PORTIA'S HOUSE

Enter LORENZO and JESSICA

LORENZO

    The moon shines bright: in such a night as this,

    When the sweet wind did gently kiss the trees,

    And they did make no noise, in such a night,

    Troilus methinks mounted the Troyan walls,

    And sigh'd his soul toward the Grecian tents,

    Where Cressid lay that night.

JESSICA

    In such a night

    Did Thisby fearfully o'ertrip the dew,

    And saw the lion's shadow ere himself,

    And ran dismay'd away.

LORENZO

    In such a night

Stood Dido with a willow in her hand
Upon the wild sea-banks, and waft her love
To come again to Carthage.

JESSICA

In such a night
Medea gather'd the enchanted herbs
That did renew old Aeson.

LORENZO

In such a night
Did Jessica steal from the wealthy Jew,
And with an unthrift love did run from Venice
As far as Belmont.

JESSICA

In such a night
Did young Lorenzo swear he lov'd her well,
Stealing her soul with many vows of faith,
And ne'er a true one.

LORENZO

In such a night
Did pretty Jessica, like a little shrew,
Slander her love, and he forgave it her.

JESSICA

I would out-night you, did no body come;
But, hark, I hear the footing of a man.

Enter STEPHANO

LORENZO

Who comes so fast in silence of the night?

STEPHANO

A friend.

LORENZO

A friend! What friend? Your name, I pray you,
friend?

STEPHANO

Stephano is my name, and I bring word
My mistress will before the break of day
Be here at Belmont; she doth stray about
By holy crosses, where she kneels and prays
For happy wedlock hours.

LORENZO

Who comes with her?

STEPHANO

None but a holy hermit and her maid.
I pray you, is my master yet return'd?

LORENZO

He is not, nor we have not heard from him.
But go we in, I pray thee, Jessica,
And ceremoniously let us prepare
Some welcome for the mistress of the house.

Enter LAUNCELOT

LAUNCELOT

Sola, sola! wo ha, ho! sola, sola!

LORENZO

Who calls?

LAUNCELOT

Sola! Did you see Master Lorenzo? Master Lorenzo! Sola, sola!

LORENZO

Leave holloaing, man. Here!

LAUNCELOT

Sola! Where? Where?

LORENZO

Here!

LAUNCELOT

Tell him there's a post come from my master with his horn full of good news; my master will be here ere morning.

Exit

LORENZO

Sweet soul, let's in, and there expect their coming.
And yet no matter; why should we go in?
My friend Stephano, signify, I pray you,
Within the house, your mistress is at hand;
And bring your music forth into the air.

Exit STEPHANO

How sweet the moonlight sleeps upon this bank!
Here will we sit and let the sounds of music
Creep in our ears; soft stillness and the night
Become the touches of sweet harmony.
Sit, Jessica. Look how the floor of heaven
Is thick inlaid with patines of bright gold;

There's not the smallest orb which thou
    behold'st
But in his motion like an angel sings,
Still quiring to the young-eyed cherubins;
Such harmony is in immortal souls;
But, whilst this muddy vesture of decay
Doth grossly close it in, we cannot hear it.
[Enter Musicians.]
Come, ho! and wake Diana with a hymn;
With sweetest touches pierce your mistress' ear,
And draw her home with music.
    [*Music*]

JESSICA

I am never merry when I hear sweet music.

LORENZO

The reason is, your spirits are attentive;
For do but note a wild and wanton herd,
Or race of youthful and unhandled colts,
Fetching mad bounds, bellowing and neighing
    loud,
Which is the hot condition of their blood;
If they but hear perchance a trumpet sound,
Or any air of music touch their ears,
You shall perceive them make a mutual stand,
Their savage eyes turn'd to a modest gaze
By the sweet power of music: therefore the
    poet

Did feign that Orpheus drew trees, stones, and
     floods;
Since nought so stockish, hard, and full of rage,
But music for the time doth change his nature.
The man that hath no music in himself,
Nor is not mov'd with concord of sweet sounds,
Is fit for treasons, stratagems, and spoils;
The motions of his spirit are dull as night,
And his affections dark as Erebus.
Let no such man be trusted. Mark the music.

Enter PORTIA and
NERISSA, at a distance.

PORTIA

That light we see is burning in my hall.
How far that little candle throws his beams!
So shines a good deed in a naughty world.

NERISSA

When the moon shone, we did not see the
candle.

PORTIA

So doth the greater glory dim the less:
A substitute shines brightly as a king
Until a king be by, and then his state
Empties itself, as doth an inland brook
Into the main of waters. Music! hark!

NERISSA

It is your music, madam, of the house.

PORTIA

> Nothing is good, I see, without respect:
> Methinks it sounds much sweeter than by day.

NERISSA

> Silence bestows that virtue on it, madam.

PORTIA

> The crow doth sing as sweetly as the lark
> When neither is attended; and I think
> The nightingale, if she should sing by day,
> When every goose is cackling, would be thought
> No better a musician than the wren.
> How many things by season season'd are
> To their right praise and true perfection!
> Peace, ho! The moon sleeps with Endymion,
> And would not be awak'd!
> [*Music ceases.*]

LORENZO

> That is the voice,
> Or I am much deceiv'd, of Portia.

PORTIA

> He knows me as the blind man knows the
>   cuckoo,
> By the bad voice.

LORENZO

> Dear lady, welcome home.

PORTIA

> We have been praying for our husbands' welfare,

Which speed, we hope, the better for our words.
Are they return'd?

LORENZO

Madam, they are not yet;
But there is come a messenger before,
To signify their coming.

PORTIA

Go in, Nerissa:
Give order to my servants that they take
No note at all of our being absent hence;
Nor you, Lorenzo; Jessica, nor you.
[*A tucket sounds.*]

LORENZO

Your husband is at hand; I hear his trumpet.
We are no tell-tales, madam, fear you not.

PORTIA

This night methinks is but the daylight sick;
It looks a little paler; 'tis a day
Such as the day is when the sun is hid.

     Enter BASSANIO, ANTONIO,
     GRATIANO, and their Followers.

BASSANIO

We should hold day with the Antipodes,
If you would walk in absence of the sun.

PORTIA

Let me give light, but let me not be light,
For a light wife doth make a heavy husband,

And never be Bassanio so for me:
But God sort all! You are welcome home, my
    lord.

BASSANIO

I thank you, madam; give welcome to my friend:
This is the man, this is Antonio,
To whom I am so infinitely bound.

PORTIA

You should in all sense be much bound to him,
For, as I hear, he was much bound for you.

ANTONIO

No more than I am well acquitted of.

PORTIA

Sir, you are very welcome to our house.
It must appear in other ways than words,
Therefore I scant this breathing courtesy.

GRATIANO

[To NERISSA]

By yonder moon I swear you do me wrong;
In faith, I gave it to the judge's clerk.
Would he were gelt that had it, for my part,
Since you do take it, love, so much at heart.

PORTIA

A quarrel, ho, already! What's the matter?

GRATIANO

About a hoop of gold, a paltry ring
That she did give me, whose posy was

For all the world like cutlers' poetry

Upon a knife, 'Love me, and leave me not.'

NERISSA

What talk you of the posy, or the value?

You swore to me, when I did give it you,

That you would wear it till your hour of death,

And that it should lie with you in your grave;

Though not for me, yet for your vehement oaths,

You should have been respective and have kept it.

Gave it a judge's clerk! No, God's my judge,

The clerk will ne'er wear hair on's face that had it.

GRATIANO

He will, an if he live to be a man.

NERISSA

Ay, if a woman live to be a man.

GRATIANO

Now, by this hand, I gave it to a youth,

A kind of boy, a little scrubbed boy

No higher than thyself, the judge's clerk;

A prating boy that begg'd it as a fee;

I could not for my heart deny it him.

PORTIA

You were to blame, I must be plain with you,

To part so slightly with your wife's first gift,

A thing stuck on with oaths upon your finger,
And so riveted with faith unto your flesh.
I gave my love a ring, and made him swear
Never to part with it, and here he stands,
I dare be sworn for him he would not leave it
Nor pluck it from his finger for the wealth
That the world masters. Now, in faith, Gratiano,
You give your wife too unkind a cause of grief;
An 'twere to me, I should be mad at it.

BASSANIO

[*Aside*] Why, I were best to cut my left hand off,
And swear I lost the ring defending it.

GRATIANO

My Lord Bassanio gave his ring away
Unto the judge that begg'd it, and indeed
Deserv'd it too; and then the boy, his clerk,
That took some pains in writing, he begg'd
      mine;
And neither man nor master would take aught
But the two rings.

PORTIA

What ring gave you, my lord?
Not that, I hope, which you receiv'd of me.

BASSANIO

If I could add a lie unto a fault,
I would deny it; but you see my finger
Hath not the ring upon it; it is gone.

PORTIA

Even so void is your false heart of truth;
By heaven, I will ne'er come in your bed
Until I see the ring.

NERISSA

Nor I in yours
Till I again see mine.

BASSANIO

Sweet Portia,
If you did know to whom I gave the ring,
If you did know for whom I gave the ring,
And would conceive for what I gave the ring,
And how unwillingly I left the ring,
When nought would be accepted but the ring,
You would abate the strength of your
displeasure.

PORTIA

If you had known the virtue of the ring,
Or half her worthiness that gave the ring,
Or your own honour to contain the ring,
You would not then have parted with the ring.
What man is there so much unreasonable,
If you had pleas'd to have defended it
With any terms of zeal, wanted the modesty
To urge the thing held as a ceremony?
Nerissa teaches me what to believe:
I'll die for't but some woman had the ring.

BASSANIO

No, by my honour, madam, by my soul,
No woman had it, but a civil doctor,
Which did refuse three thousand ducats of me,
And begg'd the ring; the which I did deny him,
And suffer'd him to go displeas'd away;
Even he that had held up the very life
Of my dear friend. What should I say, sweet lady?
I was enforc'd to send it after him;
I was beset with shame and courtesy;
My honour would not let ingratitude
So much besmear it. Pardon me, good lady;
For, by these blessed candles of the night,
Had you been there, I think you would have begg'd
The ring of me to give the worthy doctor.

PORTIA

Let not that doctor e'er come near my house;
Since he hath got the jewel that I loved,
And that which you did swear to keep for me,
I will become as liberal as you;
I'll not deny him anything I have,
No, not my body, nor my husband's bed.
Know him I shall, I am well sure of it.
Lie not a night from home; watch me like Argus;
If you do not, if I be left alone,
Now, by mine honour which is yet mine own,
I'll have that doctor for mine bedfellow.

NERISSA

And I his clerk; therefore be well advis'd

How you do leave me to mine own protection.

GRATIANO

Well, do you so: let not me take him then;

For, if I do, I'll mar the young clerk's pen.

ANTONIO

I am the unhappy subject of these quarrels.

PORTIA

Sir, grieve not you; you are welcome notwithstanding.

BASSANIO

Portia, forgive me this enforced wrong;

And in the hearing of these many friends

I swear to thee, even by thine own fair eyes,

Wherein I see myself—

PORTIA

Mark you but that!

In both my eyes he doubly sees himself,

In each eye one; swear by your double self,

And there's an oath of credit.

BASSANIO

Nay, but hear me:

Pardon this fault, and by my soul I swear

I never more will break an oath with thee.

ANTONIO

I once did lend my body for his wealth,

Which, but for him that had your husband's
    ring,
Had quite miscarried; I dare be bound again,
My soul upon the forfeit, that your lord
Will never more break faith advisedly.

PORTIA

Then you shall be his surety. Give him this,
And bid him keep it better than the other.

ANTONIO

Here, Lord Bassanio, swear to keep this ring.

BASSANIO

By heaven! it is the same I gave the doctor!

PORTIA

I had it of him: pardon me, Bassanio,
For, by this ring, the doctor lay with me.

NERISSA

And pardon me, my gentle Gratiano,
For that same scrubbed boy, the doctor's clerk,
In lieu of this, last night did lie with me.

GRATIANO

Why, this is like the mending of high ways
In summer, where the ways are fair enough.
What! are we cuckolds ere we have deserv'd it?

PORTIA

Speak not so grossly. You are all amaz'd:
Here is a letter; read it at your leisure;
It comes from Padua, from Bellario:

There you shall find that Portia was the doctor,
Nerissa there, her clerk: Lorenzo here
Shall witness I set forth as soon as you,
And even but now return'd; I have not yet
Enter'd my house. Antonio, you are welcome;
And I have better news in store for you
Than you expect: unseal this letter soon;
There you shall find three of your argosies
Are richly come to harbour suddenly.
You shall not know by what strange accident
I chanced on this letter.

ANTONIO

I am dumb.

BASSANIO

Were you the doctor, and I knew you not?

GRATIANO

Were you the clerk that is to make me cuckold?

NERISSA

Ay, but the clerk that never means to do it,
Unless he live until he be a man.

BASSANIO

Sweet doctor, you shall be my bedfellow:
When I am absent, then lie with my wife.

ANTONIO

Sweet lady, you have given me life and living;
For here I read for certain that my ships
Are safely come to road.

PORTIA

    How now, Lorenzo!

    My clerk hath some good comforts too for you.

NERISSA

    Ay, and I'll give them him without a fee.

    There do I give to you and Jessica,

    From the rich Jew, a special deed of gift,

    After his death, of all he dies possess'd of.

LORENZO

    Fair ladies, you drop manna in the way

    Of starved people.

PORTIA

    It is almost morning,

    And yet I am sure you are not satisfied

    Of these events at full. Let us go in;

    And charge us there upon inter'gatories,

    And we will answer all things faithfully.

GRATIANO

    Let it be so: he first inter'gatory

    That my Nerissa shall be sworn on is,

    Whe'r till the next night she had rather stay,

    Or go to bed now, being two hours to day:

    But were the day come, I should wish it dark,

    Till I were couching with the doctor's clerk.

    Well, while I live, I'll fear no other thing

    So sore as keeping safe Nerissa's ring.

Exeunt